The Biblical Roots of the Mass

Thomas J. Nash

The Biblical Roots
of the Mass

SOPHIA INSTITUTE PRESS
Manchester, New Hampshire

Nihil obstat: Rev. James Dunfee
Imprimatur: ✠ Bishop R. Daniel Conlon

Sophia Institute Press
Box 5284, Manchester, NH 03108
1-800-888-9344
www.SophiaInstitute.com

Sophia Institute Press® is a registered trademark of Sophia Institute.

Library of Congress Cataloging-in-Publication Data
Nash, Tom.
   [Worthy is the lamb]
   The biblical roots of the mass / Thomas J. Nash.
      pages cm
   Reprint of: Worthy is the lamb.—San Francisco : Ignatius Press, ?2004.
   Includes bibliographical references and index.
      ISBN 978-1-62282-259-1 (pbk. : alk. paper) 1. Lord's Supper—Biblical teaching. 2. Lord's Supper—Catholic Church. I. Title.
      BV825.3.N37 2015
      234'.163—dc23
                                                              2015005103

First printing

With great love to Mom and Dad,
Genevieve and Joseph Nash,
whose lifelong witness to Jesus Christ
and his Catholic Church
is further evidence that it's all true

Contents

Part III
Mass Appeal

Foreword

Two great and recent liturgical events make this book a joy to read. First, the fortieth anniversary of the publication of *Sacrosanctum Concilium* (December 4, 2003) moves us to meditate on the meaning of that full, conscious, and active participation in the celebration of the Holy Eucharist so urgently called for by the Council Fathers.[1] Second, Pope John Paul II's encyclical letter *Ecclesia de Eucharistia* (Holy Thursday, 2003) calls us to deepen our appreciation, amazement, and gratitude for the Eucharistic Mystery.

In his encyclical letter, the Holy Father wonders whether even the apostles gathered in the Upper Room understood the full meaning of the words spoken by Christ. Throughout his life, each reader of this book has sought to deepen his understanding of the *holy and living sacrifice*, which is the source of the Christian life and the summit of every good work.[2]

---

[1] Vatican II, *Sacrosanctum Concilium* ("Constitution on the Sacred Liturgy"), nos. 14, 41, 48, in Austin Flannery, O.P., ed., *Vatican Council II: The Conciliar and Post Conciliar Documents* (Northpoint, NY: Costello Publishing, 1975).

[2] See ibid., no. 10.

In this book, Thomas Nash helps us to revisit the fonts of our understanding of the Eucharistic Mystery. So we journey with him in an exploration of the many dimensions of the Catholic Faith in the Mass, "the sacrificial memorial in which the sacrifice of the Cross is perpetuated, and the sacred banquet of communion with the Lord's body and blood."[3]

Each time we gather to celebrate the sacred mysteries, may our study of the Church's teaching on the Eucharist draw us more deeply into the mysteries we celebrate. Each time we kneel in adoration before the Blessed Sacrament, may the holy teachings allow us to embrace the Eucharistic gift more fully. Each time we seek to join our lives to the great sacrifice of praise of Christ upon the Cross, may our ever-deepening understanding of Holy Communion make us ever more one with our Lord and Savior.

As our Holy Father reminds us, "the Eucharist is a *mysterium fidei*, a mystery which surpasses our understanding and can only be received in faith."[4] As we refresh our understanding of the Church's Eucharistic teaching in these pages, may God grant us the grace to be joined ever more closely to the Eucharistic Sacrifice of the Cross.

—Monsignor James Patrick Moroney
Executive Director, Secretariat for the Liturgy
United States Conference of Catholic Bishops

[3] Pope John Paul II, encyclical letter *Ecclesia de Eucharistia* ("On the Eucharist in Its Relationship to the Church"), (Boston: Pauline Books and Media, 2003), no. 12.

[4] Ibid., no. 15.

The Biblical Roots of the Mass

Introduction

Follow the Lamb
Rediscovering the Biblical Story of the Mass

At St. Mary of Redford in Detroit, the beloved parish of my youth, there is a sermon etched in stone and stained glass that aches for a well-formed and worldwide audience. St. Mary's proclaims the biblical story of the Mass within its French-Romanesque structure, a story illustrated in four windows that peer down upon the sanctuary. But it is also a story that remains hidden from the casual visitor and, more significantly, from too many Catholics in general.

From a distance, the windows' stunning beauty catches your attention. Because the sanctuary's enormous arch and associated pillars obstruct your view, however, you move forward for a closer, more informed look. When you enter a semicircular walkway that rings the sanctuary, and provided that you have "eyes to see" (see Matt. 13:10–17), you will encounter the biblical story of the Mass, the Catholic Church's liturgical heritage writ large on stained glass, for each window depicts a famous sacrifice of the Old Testament that prefigures Jesus Christ's everlasting Sacrifice of Calvary:

- Abel's sacrifice of his firstborn lambs (Gen. 4:2–4)
- Melchizedek's offering of bread and wine (Gen. 14:17–20)

- Abraham's sacrifice of Isaac (Gen. 22:1–19)

- The sacrifice of the Passover lambs, which helped liberate Israel from Egyptian bondage (Exod. 12:1–32)

As a backdrop to the altar on which Christ's Sacrifice is made sacramentally present at every Mass, the windows at St. Mary's are well placed, because they collectively portray the biblical story that culminates in the same Sacrifice that Christ first made known to us at the Last Supper.

Unfortunately, given their faith formation, many Catholics understandably do not have "eyes to see" the Mass's biblical roots, nor do they really grasp how Christ's Sacrifice can be made present throughout time. Indeed, many practicing Catholics do not really understand the biblical story of the Mass, a lack of understanding that is even more pronounced among those U.S. Catholics — more than 50 percent — who sadly do not even participate regularly in Sunday liturgy.[5] The rich meaning of God's

---

[5] The clerical sexual abuse crisis that rocked the Church in the United States in 2002 negatively impacted Mass participation and Eucharistic belief statistics among U.S. Catholics, although the Church has been rebounding. For example, a February 2003 Gallup survey found that weekly Mass participation rates had dipped to 35 percent, an all-time low since Gallup began measuring Church attendance in 1955. However, a November 2003 Gallup survey showed the weekly rate had increased to 45 percent ("Church Attendance Is Up, but Still Down," *Steubenville Register,* January 16, 2004, 1).

See also Philip F. Lawler, "A Principle Rejected," *Catholic World Report*, March 1997, 44–50. The magazine commissioned the Roper Center for Public Opinion Research to conduct a survey of Catholic belief and practice. Findings included that 56 percent of Catholics typically participate in Mass at least once a week, presumably on Sunday. On a bright note, 62 percent of the

sacrificial love remains hidden from them, and too many know too little about the liberating message of the Mass.

Like St. Mary's stained-glass story observed from a distance by a visitor, the meaning of the Mass remains obscure for many Catholics. At St. Mary's, a far-off glimpse will contribute only to an edifying memory of a lovely church. Unless visitors come forward, they will never observe, let alone begin to understand, the wonderful story that the windows proclaim. Similarly, Catholics at Mass can hear the brief, yet intriguing message that the offerings of Abel, Melchizedek, and Abraham are somehow connected with Christ's Sacrifice (Eucharistic Prayer I). However, unless they are "welcomed forward" for better instruction, the profound relationship between these Old Testament luminaries and "the Lamb of God, who takes away the sin of the world" (John 1:29) will remain tragically obscure for many of them.

All Catholics at least know that the Church teaches that Christ died for them on Calvary two thousand years ago. After all, the crucifix is probably the most well known and recognized Catholic image. But the Last Supper and Christ's death and Resurrection are often viewed by too many Catholics as vaguely important *past* events. These Catholics do not understand that

---

respondents strongly agreed with the statement that "the bread and wine used in Mass are actually transformed into the body and blood of Jesus Christ," while 20 percent mildly agreed. The Eucharistic belief findings were significantly better than those of a 1994 *New York Times*/CBS poll. However, the *Times*/CBS survey was somewhat flawed because it gave respondents a choice to identify the Eucharist as a "symbolic reminder" of Jesus Christ or as his actual Body and Blood. Such a survey more accurately measures Catholics' precise knowledge of the Faith than determining whether they affirm the Church's basic teaching on the Eucharist.

the Bible conveys a truly Catholic story in which salvation history first prefigures and then wondrously records Christ's Sacrifice of Calvary.[6] In addition, surveys have shown that a minority of Catholics do not even believe in the Real Presence of Christ in the Eucharist, although it would seem that most of these do not participate in weekly (Sunday) Mass or have not received adequate instruction on the subject,[7] or both. And many of those who do believe cannot provide a biblically based, basic explanation of how Jesus' one Self-Sacrifice is mysteriously made present at each and every Mass. We will see in this book that "the story of the Mass" is one with "the story of the Bible."

Led by the Lamb

Countless books have been written on the celebration of the Mass and its historical development, from its Jewish roots to its modern-day presentation. However, as conveyed by the *Catechism of the Catholic Church* (hereinafter CCC or the *Catechism*), the heart of the Mass will always remain the "Eucharistic celebration" (CCC 1333), the sacramental "representation" of Christ's one Sacrifice — thus the longstanding liturgical term "holy Sacrifice of the Mass" (CCC 1330). The *Catechism* (no. 1366), explains:

---

[6] I prefer to use the phrase "Sacrifice of Calvary" rather than "Sacrifice on Calvary" because the events of Jesus' Sacrifice are not limited to his suffering and death on the Cross.

[7] For example, the 1997 survey by the Roper Center for Public Opinion Research found that 5 percent mildly disagreed with the statement that "the bread and wine used in Mass are actually transformed into the body and blood of Jesus Christ," while 7 percent strongly disagreed (Lawler, "A Principle Rejected," *Catholic World Report*, March 1997, 45).

[Christ], our Lord and God, was once and for all to offer himself to God the Father by his death on the altar of the cross, to accomplish there an everlasting redemption. But because his priesthood was not to end with his death, at the Last Supper "on the night when he was betrayed," [he wanted] to leave his beloved spouse the Church a visible sacrifice (as the nature of man demands) by which the bloody sacrifice which he was to accomplish once for all on the cross would be re-presented, its memory perpetuated until the end of the world, and its salutary power be applied to the forgiveness of the sins we daily commit (Council of Trent [1562]: DS 1740; cf. 1 Cor 11:23; Heb 7:24, 27).

This present book will trace the biblical story of the Mass by following the "sacrificial lamb" motif—from the book of Genesis to the Gospels and beyond.

Lambs usually follow. But the biblical story of the Mass is all about following the sacrificial lamb, from Abel's worthy offering, to the lambs offered and eaten during the celebration of Passover, to the One who laid down his life for the world. It is the sacrifice of this same Lamb—Jesus himself—that the Church makes present and partakes of at every Mass, the new Passover (see CCC 1362–1365)! The Church tells the story in summary form at Mass in Eucharistic Prayer I. After consecrating the bread and wine so it becomes the Body and Blood of Jesus—that is, the Sacrament of the Eucharist—the priest prays to our Father in heaven:

> Therefore, O Lord,
> as we celebrate the memorial of the blessed
> Passion,

the Resurrection from the dead,
and the glorious Ascension into heaven
of Christ, your Son, our Lord,
we, your servants and your holy people,
offer to your glorious majesty
from the gifts that you have given us,
this pure victim,
this holy victim,
this spotless victim,
the holy Bread of eternal life
and the Chalice of everlasting salvation.

Be pleased to look upon these offerings
with a serene and kindly countenance,
and to accept them,
as once you were pleased to accept
the gifts of your servant Abel the just,
the sacrifice of Abraham, our father in faith,
and the offering of your high priest
    Melchizedek,
a holy sacrifice, a spotless victim.

In humble prayer we ask you, almighty God:
command that these gifts be borne
by the hands of your holy Angel
to your altar on high
in the sight of your divine majesty,
so that all of us, who through this participation
    at the altar
receive the most holy Body and Blood of your
    Son,

may be filled with every grace and heavenly blessing. Through Christ our Lord. Amen.[8]

Eucharistic Prayer I is rich with catechetical substance. Yet we in the Church need to find better ways to convey this rich teaching in both Sunday liturgies and elsewhere, because too many Catholics are either not participating in Mass or participating without adequate formation. As the Ethiopian eunuch said, "How can I [understand], unless someone guides me?" (Acts 8:31).

The architecture of St. Mary's provides us with direction, reminding us that all effective catechesis begins and ends with Jesus. The four windows flank an imposing statue of Mary with the Infant Jesus, whose sheer size, accompanying lighting, and central location just behind the sanctuary immediately grab your attention when you enter the church. It is as if our Lady, true to form, leads us to Jesus—not away from him. She initially draws our gaze, only to focus our eyes on her beloved Son, cradled in her arms. Why the focus on Jesus? The windows tell the story. Adam and Eve's original sin ruptured mankind's communion with God, while the various sacrifices depicted in the windows advanced the cause of restoring that precious communion. For the discerning observer, the windows explain how God prepared and made provision for his Son's ultimate restoration on our behalf, fulfilling the work begun by Abel, Melchizedek, Abraham, the Passover, and all of the Temple sacrifices.

Jesus came to earth to become both perfect priest and victim, and so our eyes at St. Mary's move from the statue of the Infant Jesus, to the windows, back to the Infant Jesus, and then down to

---

[8] International Commission on English in the Liturgy, *The Roman Missal*, 3rd typical ed. (New York: Catholic Book Publishing, 2010), Eucharistic Prayer I (Roman Canon).

the altar, the sacred table on which the Church commemorates and re-presents his *one*, perfect Sacrifice at every Mass:

> The presentation of the offerings at the altar takes up the gesture of Melchizedek and commits the Creator's gifts into the hands of Christ who, in his sacrifice, *brings to perfection all human attempts to offer sacrifices.* (CCC 1350, emphasis added)[9]

Where did Christ first "take up" the gestures of Melchizedek, mysteriously offering his Body and Blood under the appearances of bread and wine? At the Last Supper. What Christ first "pre-presented" and anticipated at the Last Supper in mystery[10] and

---

[9] In its "Doctrine Concerning the Sacrifice of the Mass," chap. 2, the Council of Trent teaches that Christ fulfills all Old Testament offerings in instituting the Sacrifice of the Mass: "It is, finally, that [sacrifice] which was prefigured by various types of sacrifices during the period of nature and of the law, which, namely, comprises all the good things signified by them, as being the consummation and perfection of them all"; as cited in *The Canons and Decrees of the Council of Trent*, trans. Rev. H. J. Schroeder, O.P. (Rockford, IL: TAN Books, 1978), 145, footnote omitted.

[10] See CCC 610–611. At the Last Supper, Jesus' "giving" of his Body to his disciples and speaking of the "shedding" of his Blood "do indeed announce an imminent death.... The man who is about to die is disposing of the future: death will certainly bring separation, but from it will come the covenant that unites the disciples to God in Jesus who has rejoined the Father. In the new universe thus inaugurated, in the space that is opened up yet left empty by the Master's departure, Jesus will himself be their bread and their cup as long as the present world lasts.... This man who is about to die but is already master of the future leaves his presence in advance as a legacy; it will be an active presence among his followers and will make them active in their

told us to continue "in memory" of him, he also lived out on Calvary in history.

This is a crucial part of the biblical story of the Mass, one that *needs* to be proclaimed regularly and explained well. The whole Church—the whole world—needs to know that the Last Supper was not simply a symbolic precursor of Christ's redemptive suffering on Calvary. Rather, these two historical events actually encompass *one* divine and mysterious Sacrifice that impacts all of salvation history, and that is why we can continue—two thousand years later—to re-present and celebrate that same Sacrifice at every Mass (see CCC 1366–1367).

Contrary to what some Christians believe, Catholics do not try to recrucify Jesus at every Mass. Rather, as will be explained in detail, the Church re-presents in the Mass Christ's *completed* Sacrifice of Calvary, a Sacrifice he culminated in *everlasting* glory at his Ascension, when he presented himself on our behalf to his Father in the heavenly sanctuary (Heb. 9:23–24). As we will see, and as the words "everlasting glory" imply, Jesus continues to present his completed Sacrifice of Calvary in heaven, because he holds his priesthood permanently (Heb. 7:23–25).

The Second Vatican Council describes the Sacrifice of the Mass as "the source and summit of the Christian life."[11] The Mass is a Sacrifice so powerful and so time-transcendent that our brothers and sisters in heaven can celebrate it with us "without [sacramental] signs," for "liturgy is an 'action' of the *whole* Christ

---

turn" (Fr. Xavier Léon-Dufour, S.J., *Sharing the Eucharistic Bread: The Witness of the New Testament,* trans. Matthew O'Connell [Mahwah, NJ: Paulist Press, 1987], 61–62).

[11] Vatican II, *Lumen Gentium* ("Dogmatic Constitution on the Church"), no. 11, as cited in Flannery, *Vatican Council II,* 362. See Vatican II, *Sacrosanctum Concilium,* no. 10, as cited in ibid., 6.

(*Christus totus*)" (CCC 1136, emphasis in original). The saints in heaven benefit from seeing God face-to-face, but join us in proclaiming God's glory: "Worthy is the Lamb who was slain, for thou wast slain, ... and by thy blood didst ransom men for God from every tribe and tongue and people and nation, and hast made them a kingdom and priests to our God, and they shall reign on earth" (Rev. 5:12, 9–10; see 5:6–14).

Thus, while some view the Eucharistic Sacrifice of the Mass as a stumbling block to ecumenism and to worldwide evangelization, the Catholic Church understands that the Mass is indispensable to achieving her divinely ordained mandate:

> The Church's mission stands in continuity with the mission of Christ: "As the Father has sent me, even so I send you" (Jn 20:21). From the perpetuation of the sacrifice of the Cross and her communion with the body and blood of Christ in the Eucharist, the Church draws the spiritual power needed to carry out her mission. The Eucharist thus appears as both *the source* and *the summit* of all evangelization, since its goal is the communion of mankind with Christ and in him with the Father and the Holy Spirit.[12]

God "desires all men to be saved" (1 Tim. 2:4; see 2 Pet. 3:9), and therefore the biblical story of the Mass, the story of salvation history, is a story for all mankind. May we learn it and live it well, so that we can better participate in Christ's saving mission.

---

[12] Pope John Paul II, encyclical letter *Ecclesia de Eucharistia* (Boston: Pauline Books and Media, 2003), no. 22, italics in original, footnote omitted. This encyclical is available online at http://www.vatican.va.

Questions for Reflection or Group Discussion

1. For many centuries, before the invention of the printing press, most people in the world could not read. Therefore, in addition to preaching the Word of God, the Church used art to teach the faithful. St. Mary of Redford's beautiful stained-glass windows continue to illustrate the profound storytelling ability of religious art. (a) What church buildings in your area tell well the biblical story of the Mass or the Catholic Faith in general? Have you ever considered an evangelistic trip with a friend to such a church? How about a trip to a display of Catholic art at a nearby museum? (b) Do you proclaim your faith with religious images at home, adorning your house with crucifixes and other Catholic images, including paintings? (c) Do you take advantage of religious art in sharing the Faith with your family and friends? In what ways?

2. St. Mary's has grouped the activities of Abel, Abraham, and the Passover together in its sanctuary. (a) What can we initially see in common between the three events? (b) Melchizedek is also featured at St. Mary's. How is his action basically similar to the other three? (Hint: What is the prime function of a priest? See Heb. 5:1). How is his action different? (c) What early, fundamental connection can we draw between the sacrificial similarities of these four offerings? (Hint: see Eucharistic Prayer I excerpt.)

3. (a) Why do you think Vatican II called the Mass "the source and summit of the Christian life"? (b) Explain Pope John Paul II's more particular statement that the Eucharistic Sacrifice is "*the source* and *the summit*" of all evangelization."

Part 1

Genesis of the Eucharist

1

In God We Trust?

Paradise Last

Background Reading
  Genesis 2–3
  Catechism of the Catholic Church, nos. 388–397

The story of the Mass begins in the Garden of Eden. Adam and Eve had a basic choice: listen to the devil and become "like God" (Gen. 3:5) or listen to God and partake of his very life.

"You may freely eat of every tree of the garden," God told Adam and Eve. "[B]ut of the tree of the knowledge of good and evil you shall not eat, for in the day that you eat of it you shall die" (Gen. 2:16–17).

Meanwhile, the devil assured our first parents that eating of that tree would make them "be like God, knowing good and evil" (Gen. 3:5).

Contrary to what some secular humanists and other scriptural cynics maintain, God was not demanding blind and foolish obedience from the first man and woman. He endowed both Adam and Eve with an intellect to understand and a will to make choices. He gave them a choice to serve him freely, the same choice he had given the devil and his angelic confreres. In giving them such freedom, God truly loved Adam and Eve, because true love necessarily implies freedom, while love coerced is no love at all.

For his part, the devilish serpent (see Rev. 12:9) had chosen badly, and he was quite willing to exploit any doubts our first parents might have, thereby illustrating early on in human history that misery likes company (see CCC 391–395). The devil did not like being told what to do, and he thought he might similarly persuade Adam and Eve to reject conformity with the Almighty. Would they be docile, obedient sheep, or would Adam and Eve be "independent-minded" goats and go their own way? The forbidden fruit of Eden, then, was a matter of trust. The Hebrew word *know* in Genesis 3:5 and 3:22 is *yada*, which means "knowledge or understanding gained by experience." Would Adam and Eve trust God and the knowledge he gave them, or would they seek independent verification on their own?

To trust God is to demonstrate hope in him (see CCC 1817), but Adam and Eve turned away from God and disobeyed him, reaping a bitter harvest from their original sin that would deal death to both them and all of their descendants (see CCC 402–406).

Ironically, God provided our first parents an opportunity to choose life, and not simply by abstaining from the tree of the knowledge of good and evil. He gave them various trees from which they could "freely eat," yet he bothered to name only one: "the tree of life" (Gen. 2:9). God told Adam and Eve that the forbidden tree would bear fruit that brings only death, so why didn't they seek refuge in the tree that would apparently provide just the opposite—life? That remains somewhat of a mystery, although a lack of trust in God's goodness and providence, as in all sin, played a key role (see CCC 387, 397–398). The Church teaches that Adam and Eve possessed immortality through the gift of "original holiness" (see CCC 375–376), but they were also given the choice to reject that gift. Adam and Eve chose to turn away from God, and paradise was lost.

An Invitation to Eternal Life

Jesus came to restore paradise, to do what the first Adam failed to do, to give us another opportunity to partake of eternal life. He did so by sacrificing himself for our sins, dying on the Cross, and then rising on Easter Sunday:

> Christ has been raised from the dead, the first fruits of those who have fallen asleep. For as by a man came death, by a man has come also the resurrection of the dead. For as in Adam all die, so also in Christ shall all be *made alive* (1 Cor. 15:20–22, emphasis added).

> A tree [of the knowledge of good and evil] brought death, life is from the Cross.[13]

Christ "makes us alive" through his sacraments (see CCC 1131), beginning with Baptism, but in an ongoing manner through the Eucharist: "[H]e who eats my flesh and drinks my blood has eternal life, and I will raise him up at the last day. For my flesh is food indeed, and my blood is drink indeed" (John 6:54–55).[14]

---

[13] St. Ambrose, as cited in Jean Daniélou, S.J., *From Shadows to Reality: Studies in the Biblical Typology of the Fathers* (London: Burns and Oates, 1960), 46.

[14] See Pope John Paul II, *Ecclesia de Eucharistia*, no. 18.

There are other intriguing connections between the life of Adam and the Eucharistic work of Jesus. In Genesis 3:22 God conveys that, if Adam had chosen the fruit of the tree of life instead of that of the tree of the knowledge of good and evil, Adam would have "eaten and lived for ever." In John 6:58, Jesus tells the world that what Adam forsook is now available again, because to "eat and live for ever" now applies to him, the Bread come down from heaven.[15] In addition, when Adam and Eve ate the forbidden fruit, "the eyes of both were opened" to their sin (Gen. 3:7).

In contrast, when Christ apparently broke Eucharistic Bread with two disciples on the road to Emmaus, "their eyes were opened and they recognized him" (Luke 24:31), the fulfilled tree of life, who would provide eternal life.[16] Jesus then vanished from his disciples' presence, apparently to impress upon them his enduring, sacramental Presence in the Eucharistic Bread.[17] "Their

---

[15] See M.-É. Boismard, *Moses or Jesus: An Essay in Johannine Christology*, trans. B. T. Viviano (Philadelphia: Fortress Press, 1993), 76–79.

[16] See Joseph Cardinal Ratzinger, *The Spirit of the Liturgy*, trans. John Saward (San Francisco: Ignatius Press, 2000), 120–121. Pope John Paul II affirms in *Ecclesia de Eucharistia*, no. 6, "To contemplate Christ involves being able to recognize him wherever he manifests himself, in his many forms of presence, but above all in the living sacrament of his body and his blood.... Whenever the Church celebrates the Eucharist, the faithful can in some way relive the experience of the two disciples on the road to Emmaus: 'Their eyes were opened and they recognized him'" (Luke 24:31).

[17] Christian tradition commonly holds that Jesus celebrated the first post-Resurrection Mass on the road to Emmaus with the two disciples. St. Augustine, among many others, espouses this view, although other scholars, particularly more modern ones, disagree.

eyes were not opened of their own accord; someone opened them," writes Fr. François-Xavier Durrwell, distinguishing the eye-opening process on the road to Emmaus from that which took place in Eden. "It is the Lord who, of his own accord, is present, and that Presence produces faith. It is up to man to allow himself to be opened up."[18] Indeed, the Emmaus encounter signified that Christ's visible human presence would soon no longer be needed on earth to carry out his saving mission (Luke 24:30–35; see CCC 1329, 1347).

The fruit of the tree of life is a prophetic symbol that points forward to the Eucharist, so what the Lord basically offered to Adam and Eve in Eden he offers to all of us today at the altar. In other words, you can partake of paradise down the street at your local parish.

But to partake of the tree of life, Christ adds later, one must "conquer" (Rev. 2:7). Adam and Eve mysteriously failed to conquer sin and Satan and so could not partake of the tree's fruit. Recall too that Christ is also the fulfilled Passover Lamb of God (see 1 Cor. 5:7–8), of whom we are invited to partake. To partake of the Old Covenant Passover, the Israelites had to conquer the pain of circumcision (see Exod. 12:43–49). Similarly, before we can partake of the Eucharist, we must reject sin and Satan, and not simply at our Baptism, but every time we approach the

---

See R. Ginns, O.P., "The Gospel of Jesus Christ according to St. Luke," in Dom Bernard Orchard, et al., eds., *A Catholic Commentary on Holy Scripture* (New York: Thomas Nelson and Sons, 1953), 969–970 (no. 774c). The *Catechism*, in nos. 1346–1347, provides support for a Eucharistic reading of the "road to Emmaus" account, as does CCC 1329.

[18] François-Xavier Durrwell, C.Ss.R., "Eucharist and Parousia," *Lumen Vitae* 26 (1971): 294.

Blessed Sacrament, lest we partake of it in a gravely unworthy manner (see 1 Cor. 11:27–34).

Partaking of the Eucharist does not automatically guarantee eternal life in heaven. Freedom to break communion with the Lord remains throughout our lives. As he called Adam and Eve, God calls us to a radical, childlike trust and obedience (Mark 10:15), like docile, obedient lambs who do not waver amid any tribulation they face. Although Adam and Eve initially went their own way and passed death on to us, the Good Shepherd has given us an opportunity to follow him to salvation (see Matt. 25:31–46).

Let's examine salvation history and see why lambs are worth offering *and* imitating, serving as both sacrificial paradigms and quintessential role models of discipleship. It's a matter of eternal life or death.

Questions for Reflection or Group Discussion

1. (a) What was the basic choice that God presented Adam and Eve? (b) In presenting this basic choice, why did God prohibit Adam and Eve from eating of the tree of the knowledge of good and evil? (c) What were the consequences of their decision?

2. God presented a tree to Adam and Eve that could be construed as a sign of hope and help. (a) What was the name of this tree? (b) Compare this tree's fruit with that of the tree of the knowledge of good and evil. (c) What or who could be called a tree of life in the New Testament? (d) Compare Jesus with Eden's tree of life. (e) In what ways does Jesus provide eternal life?

3. Adam and Eve failed to trust God in the Garden of Eden. (a) Do we trust God in our lives? (b) In times of crisis, do we turn and run to Jesus, the fulfilled tree of life? (c) Concretely, what must we "conquer" to partake of the fruit of the fulfilled tree of life, that is, the Eucharist?

2

Worthy Is the Lamb?

Background Reading
  Matthew 27:11–50
  Matthew 18:10–14
  John 10:1–15
  Exodus 12:1–11
  Isaiah 52:13–53:12

Even among animals, a lamb is not a likely "leading man" for a Hollywood action-adventure. Mighty Mouse or Underdog could save the day, but not a lamb; lambs are known for *needing* help in times of trouble. Recall the wandering lamb who had to be rescued (Matt. 18:12–13) or other lambs who needed protection from a menacing wolf (John 10:11–12).

What was God thinking when he chose the lamb as his ideal model of sacrifice and victory over slavery and sin?

If we were casting a hero from the animal kingdom, we would probably choose someone like the aforementioned Mighty Mouse or Underdog (for an animated feature), or Lassie or Rin Tin Tin (if we needed a real, live animal). And let's not forget the indomitable King Kong, who was especially impressive when he staved off the favored Godzilla in their epic, big-screen battle.

In any event, we surely would not cast a lamb. Lambs are cuddly and cute, but they do not exactly inspire battlefield confidence.

Jesus did not inspire confidence either as the Romans led him to his Crucifixion. He seemed to lack the militant spirit of a captured hero planning his escape. Rather, the self-professed Messiah, the designated "Lamb of God, who takes away the sin of the world" (John 1:29), was apparently meeting an untimely and most humiliating death:

> And those who passed by derided him, wagging their heads and saying, "You who would destroy the temple and build it in three days, save yourself! If you are the Son of God, come down from the cross." So also the chief priests, with the scribes and elders, mocked him, saying, "He saved others; he cannot save himself. He is the King of Israel; let him come down now from the cross, and we will believe in him. He trusts in God; let God deliver him now, if he desires him; for he said, 'I am the Son of God.'" And the robbers who were crucified with him also reviled him in the same way. (Matt 27:39–44)

Jesus' opponents thought he was just another typical "lamb," loyally following an alleged heavenly plan that had gone very wrong.

"Lamb of God?" they might have rhetorically asked. "More like a 'sham of God.'"

But this Lamb was different. While he visibly played the role of suffering servant, opening not his mouth "like a lamb that is led to the slaughter" (Isa. 53:7), Jesus simultaneously served as the triumphant Lamb of God, who won a decisive victory over sin and Satan (see Heb. 2:14–15; 1 John 3:8). Just as his jeering opponents were counting him out, just when his suffering and death seemed to signal a certain and bitter defeat, Jesus, ironically and mysteriously, became most triumphant:

> [W]hen he makes himself an offering for sin,... he shall see the fruit of the travail of his soul and be satisfied; by his knowledge shall the righteous one, my servant, make many to be accounted righteous; and he shall bear their iniquities.... [He] was numbered with the transgressors; yet he bore the sin of many, and made intercession for the transgressors. (Isa. 53:10–12; see CCC 601)

> For it was fitting that he, for whom and by whom all things exist, in bringing many sons to glory, should make the pioneer of their salvation perfect through suffering.... In the days of his flesh, Jesus offered up prayers and supplications, with loud cries and tears, to him who was able to save him from death, and he was heard for his godly fear. Although he was a Son, he learned obedience through what he suffered; *and being made perfect he became the source of eternal salvation to all who obey him,* being designated by God a high priest after the order of Melchizedek (Heb 2:10; 5:7–10, emphasis added; see CCC 608–609).

Follow the Leader

Jesus proclaimed himself "the way, the truth and the life" (John 14:6) and backed it up by rising from the dead. He also called himself "the good shepherd," adding, "I know my own and my own know me" (John 10:14). Yet our modern world resists following the Good Shepherd, in part because of the stigma attached to being a sheep.

Sheep have long had a reputation for being dumb. Ask anyone who has worked with them: sheep do not adapt and improvise;

they just follow. While goats display intelligence and independence, lambs docilely allow their shepherd to think for them. And here we need to make an important distinction. As Scripture reminds us, both young sheep and young goats[19] are lambs, and God told Moses that either would be acceptable for the original Passover sacrifice (Exod. 12:5). Yet, the docility of the sheep lamb would eventually win out over the independence of the goat lamb in salvation history. In a sobering forecast of the Last Judgment, Jesus says that the "sheep" will stand on his right and be saved, while the "goats" will stand on his left and be damned for all eternity (see Matt. 25:31–46).

Contrary to popular opinion, everyone follows someone or something. The "goats" travel down a road well worn by Satan and his fallen angelic associates, spiritual beings far more intelligent than they. "Claiming to be wise" like Satan, the goats also risk "becoming [everlasting] fools" (Rom. 1:22). Meanwhile, the "sheep" do not mind charges of "blind obedience," because they realize that their Shepherd is no ordinary person in *Who's Who*, but rather the divine "I am who I am" (Exod. 3:14; see John 8:58). While the road that leads to eternal life is narrow and hard (see Matt. 7:13–14), they understand that it reaps abundant life, now and forever (see John 10:10), and they further realize that the Good Shepherd never asks us to do anything that he has not already done himself, namely, embrace his Cross.

As the first Passover lambs gave their blood for the ransom of Israel from Egyptian slavery, "Christ, our [ultimate] paschal lamb," shed his blood to free us from sin (1 Cor. 5:7–8; see Isa. 53:10–12). He offered himself for us who had gone astray and still go astray (see CCC 615). He also offered us a lesson in living. Suffering is

---

[19] Today, a young goat is more likely to be called a kid.

not bad — in fact, it is redemptive and empowering — as long as you are suffering on behalf of God and his Kingdom.

If we suffer for the Kingdom, we can never lose, only gain. We may look like defeated sacrificial lambs, but, now and forever, we will win, just as Jesus defeated sin and death on Mount Calvary, and just as many saints have similarly laid down their lives and won ever since. As we shall see in examining the biblical record, for one reason or another, all of the sacrificial lambs were judged worthy by God, provided they were offered by those who obediently follow the Lord (see, for example, 1 Sam. 15:22). When we are willing to die to ourselves and submit to God's plan for our lives, we will ironically receive abundant life like never before. St. Paul says it best when commenting on his battles with the devil and other enemies of God's Kingdom:

> Three times I besought the Lord about this, that it should leave me; but he said to me, "My grace is sufficient for you, for my power is made perfect in weakness." I will all the more gladly boast of my weaknesses, that the power of Christ may rest upon me. For the sake of Christ, then, I am content with weaknesses, insults, hardships, persecutions, and calamities; for when I am weak, then I am strong (2 Cor. 12:9–10).

The source of Paul's strength is Jesus, the same Jesus whose Melchizedekian priesthood is mysteriously connected, as we learned above, with his becoming "the source of eternal salvation" by offering his body and blood, soul, and divinity on Calvary. How? As we will examine in more depth in subsequent chapters, Jesus allows us to re-present and partake of his *one* everlasting Sacrifice at *every* Mass under the appearances of bread and wine, that is, in a Melchizedekian fashion, just as he pre-presented and anticipated that same Sacrifice at the Last Supper, the first Mass, with his apostles. In an earlier letter to the Corinthians, Paul indicates that the Eucharist is a crucial source of strength for Christians. The Communion Bread and Cup is a blessing because we partake of the Body and Blood of Christ, which unites all Christians (1 Cor. 10:16–17).

To be found worthy like the Lamb, St. Paul teaches, we have to partake of the Lamb. We need to learn the biblical story of the Mass, but, most importantly, we need to live it.

Questions for Reflection or Group Discussion

1. In sports, teams named after sheep are called "Rams," given the strength and power the name evokes. They are called "lambs" only in ridicule, that is, when they play poorly and are "slaughtered." In addition, as Scripture conveys elsewhere, lambs are vulnerable and need to be protected. (a) In light of these considerations, modern and ancient, what was your first impression of God's choice of the lamb as a paradigm of sacrifice and heroic discipleship? (b) Did you think of any alternatives from the animal kingdom? C'mon, be honest.

2. (a) Why might some of Jesus' opponents, and even some of his followers, have erroneously viewed him as another misguided lamb? (b) What can Scripture tell us about why God chose a lamb to prefigure his Son? (See Isa. 52:13–Isa. 53:12.) (c) In speaking about his own trials, does St. Paul exemplify any attributes of the worthy, suffering Lamb? (See 2 Cor. 12:9–10.)

3. (a) How has Scripture influenced the modern metaphorical use of the term *goat*, for example, the "scapegoat"? (b) In contrast, based on the brief presentation in this chapter, why is a "sheep"

an ideal follower of Jesus? (c) Although you may be a professed follower of Christ, do you sometimes become unworthy, failing to give witness to Christ? (d) How do you strive to be worthy in your witness?

4. St. Paul speaks paradoxically when he says that he became his strongest while he was his weakest. (a) What do you think St. Paul meant? (b) Can you identify with St. Paul in your personal life? Has following Christ caused you significant suffering on occasion, only to lead to your being strengthened and renewed? (c) Can you think of any examples from the lives of the saints, such as St. Peter, St. Thomas More, and St. Maximilian Kolbe? (d) How did Jesus become his "strongest" at his "weakest"? That is, while he was on earth, how did Jesus manifest his greatest power at his weakest point?

3

Firstfruits First

Are We Willing Like Abel?

Background Reading
 Genesis 4:1–16
 John 2:13–17
 Luke 12:13–21
 Matthew 16:24–27
 Matthew 6:30–33

When I first heard about the story of Cain and Abel as a young boy, I thought I understood why God preferred Abel's sacrifice over Cain's. Abel's real, living lamb was certainly more valuable than Cain's fruits and vegetables, I thought, especially if the offering included lima beans. You see, I didn't fully understand it then, but I knew enough about the Mass to know that sacrifices were often eaten, and I also knew that lima beans were one of my least favorite foods. If Cain offered lima beans, little wonder God wasn't pleased. Something tells me that lima beans started growing only *after* the Fall. Original Sin must have permeated the soil somehow.

On a more serious note, I also felt sympathy for Cain. While his murder of Abel could never be justified, I also thought that

Cain could not help that he was a farmer and not a shepherd. Couldn't God have given Cain at least a piece of the shepherding business, so his offering would be found worthy too? It was seemingly self-evident to me that a lamb was more special than fruits and vegetables, even if any lima beans were removed.

But I also knew from faith and reason that God can do only good, so I never lost faith over the issue, although I wish I could have somehow lost out on some lima beans during my youth. In time, I took a more insightful look at this story that the Church has memorialized in the Mass:

> In the course of time Cain brought an offering of the fruit of the ground, and Abel brought of *the firstlings* of his flock and of their fat portions. And the Lord had regard for Abel and his offering, but for Cain and his offering he had no regard (Gen. 4:3–5, emphasis added).

Abel gave his firstfruits in thanksgiving to his Creator, while Cain disrespected God. Cain provided only "an offering," not the most important one: the firstfruits of his harvest. Worse yet, Cain compounded his misdeed with envy (see CCC 2539) and then murder. Like his parents, Adam and Eve, Cain did not learn the lesson of seeking God first, of placing God above himself and his perceived ability to be self-sufficient. God had given him everything, including his very existence, yet Cain did not trust God and sought his own welfare first, as if God would somehow shortchange him or that Cain would be able to make it on his own.

In contrast, Abel serves as an example for all of us. His lamb was found worthy because it was a "firstling." What we do with our firstfruits, whether financially or otherwise, speaks volumes about our priorities. God demands our firstfruits not for his sake but for ours, so that we won't go astray in a vain attempt at self-sustenance and self-fulfillment. Once again, the way of the goat can be very attractive, but the faithful, suffering sheep lamb is the one who paradoxically finds true liberation:

> If any man would come after me, let him deny himself and take up his cross and follow me. For whoever would save his life will lose it, and whoever loses his life for my sake will find it. For what will it profit a man, if he gains the whole world and forfeits his life? (Matt. 16:24–26)

Abel established a standard for salvation history, a sacrificial blueprint. *Firstfruits* signified the most important, the best, and from here on out, nothing but the best would suffice, whether Abraham's offering of Isaac, his firstborn son according to the covenant (Gen. 22:2) or God's accepting only unblemished lambs for the Passover sacrifice. Jesus Christ would fulfill all of the types, for he is both only-begotten Son and unblemished Lamb of God. In counteracting the unfaithful choice of his parents and suffering unjustly for his faithful witness, Abel himself also prefigures Jesus as the obedient, new Adam. Whereas Adam and Eve's choice barred mankind from the tree of life, Jesus laid down his life that *we* might partake of *his* sacrificial firstfruits, the eternal life-giving substance known as the Eucharist.

Abel, like Jesus, gave his best to God, even if it meant giving his own life. Firstfruits first. May we be willing like Abel.

Questions for Reflection or Group Discussion

1. (a) What was the crucial reason why God had regard for Abel's offering, but not Cain's? (b) What was Cain's initial sin toward Abel? (c) Why does the Church regard Cain's sin as a deadly sin? (See CCC 2538–2539.) (d) What does the Church

prescribe for the temptation toward Cain's sin? (See CCC 2540, 2553–2554.)

2. (a) Do I offer God and his Church my firstfruits in terms of time, money, and so on? That is, do I strive to seek and honor God in every aspect of my life? How could I witness to my family and friends in this area? (b) Do I have a daily prayer life of some sort? If I'm married, is my family involved? (c) Has my job, hobby, some relationship, or something else crowded in on my primary commitments to God and family?

3. (a) How does Abel provide an example for each one of us? (b) What does Jesus say about seeking him first through embracing the Cross? (See Matt. 16:24–26; 6:33.)

4. (a) How do Abel's example and sacrifice prefigure others in salvation history? (b) How does Abel himself prefigure Christ?

5. (a) How has my faith been tested and strengthened in seeking God first? (b) What can I share with others from my own trials and blessings as a follower of Christ?

4

Bread and Wine and
without Beginning or End
The Mysterious Priesthood of Melchizedek

Background Reading
   Genesis 14:11–20
   Hebrews 5:1–10
   Genesis 9:18–28; 10:15–20; 11:10–27; 12:1–3
   Psalm 110:1–4
   Exodus 40:12–15
   Numbers 1:47–54; 2:5–10; 3:9–10; 18:7
   Nehemiah 7:61, 64–65
   Numbers 4:1–3, 23
   Hebrews 7; 9:23–24

In celebrating Mass with gifts of bread and wine, we know that the Catholic Church takes her inspiration from Jesus, who at the Last Supper offered his Body and Blood under the sacramental forms of bread and wine, saying, "Do this in remembrance of me" (Luke 22:19).

But where did Jesus get the idea? Bread and wine were part of the Passover meal tradition that Jesus celebrated at the Last

Supper, but sacrificial lambs were the main course at this annual Israelite feast. When did God establish a biblical precedent in which bread and wine were served as a sacrificial meal? And why would Jesus, "the Lamb of God, who takes away the sin of the world" (John 1:29), associate bread and wine with a sacrificial offering of himself?

The New Testament Letter to the Hebrews provides some clues. In chapter 5 of this letter, we learn that Jesus became "the source of eternal salvation" through his Sacrifice on Calvary. By his Father he was designated "a high priest after the order of Melchizedek" (Heb. 5:9–10).[20]

Jesus' Priestly Predecessor

Who was Melchizedek? He was an ancient high priest, the first person in the Bible to offer a sacrifice of bread and wine. Melchizedek makes a brief but significant appearance in the book of Genesis (Gen. 14:17–20), commanding the attention of Abram, who would become known as Abraham, "the father of a multitude of nations" (Gen. 17:4–5). God promised to bless all nations through Abraham's descendants (see Gen.

---

[20] "Since the New Testament interprets the death of Jesus as atonement (e.g., 1 Cor. 15:3) and links the Eucharist to his death, there must have been from the start some link between Eucharist and atonement.... In the Letter to the Hebrews, for example, Christ is presented as the high priest offering the atonement sacrifice [on the Day of Atonement], and this surely should be taken as the starting point for any investigation into roots of the Christian Liturgy" (Dr. Margaret Barker, "The Temple Roots of the Liturgy," as given at http://www.marquette.edu/maqom/Roots. pdf; Barker is a British Protestant Bible scholar). For more on the link between Christ's Melchizedekian priesthood, the Eucharist and atonement, see especially chapters 7, 9, and 12 of this book.

12:1–3), which include Jesus, as the opening verse of Matthew's Gospel neatly summarizes: "Jesus Christ, the son of David, the son of Abraham" (Matt. 1:1). If Abraham, our father in faith, is listening to this mysterious Melchizedek, he must be pretty important.

Melchizedek makes his appearance right after Abram scores a major victory over several kings. Despite his battlefield triumph, Abram pays homage to Melchizedek, not vice versa:

> After [Abram's] return from the defeat of Ched-or-laomer and the kings who were with him, the king of Sodom went out to meet him at the Valley of Shaveh (that is, the King's Valley). And Melchizedek king of Salem *brought out bread and wine*; he was priest of God Most High. And he blessed him and said,
>> "Blessed be Abram by God Most High,
>>> maker of heaven and earth;
>> and blessed be God Most High,
>>> who has delivered your enemies into your hand!"
> And Abram gave him a tenth of everything
> (Gen. 14:17–20, emphasis added)

Some have questioned the nature of Melchizedek's priesthood. Because bread and wine were not the sacrificial "rite stuff" of any prominent Old Covenant sacrifices — for example, Passover and the Day of Atonement — they conclude that bread and wine could not have been the signature sacrifice of Melchizedek's priesthood. However, while proclaiming Melchizedek a great high priest, the Bible never associates his priesthood with an offering other than bread and wine. In addition, because offering sacrifice is the primary function of a priest (see Heb. 5:1–4), drawing attention to bread and wine in Genesis 14 makes little sense if Melchizedek's priesthood were distinguished by the offering of something else.

The New Testament provides clarity on the matter. As noted, Jesus offers his Body and Blood under the sacramental forms of bread and wine at the Last Supper, the first Mass. He also commands his apostles to continue this "New Covenant" tradition as a remembrance of him (Luke 22:19–20), and history records that the early Church dutifully did this. St. Paul teaches that the bread and wine Christians consume is actually a partaking of Christ's Body and Blood (see 1 Cor. 10:14–22). Indeed, the Bible illustrates that Christ's priesthood *continues* according to the order of Melchizedek, for we plainly see from St. Paul's testimony that the early Church associated Christ's Body and Blood with bread and wine, the same rite stuff that first distinguished Melchizedek's *sacrifice*. The Church continues this biblical tradition in Masses today (see CCC 1362–1377), but let us not get ahead of our story.

The Mysterious Melchizedek

Who is this mysterious and intriguing priest-king, and what was his mission? The *Catechism* mentions Melchizedek in four paragraphs (nos. 58, 1333, 1350, 1544). He is listed as a Gentile in paragraph 58. Before Abraham, the Hebrew patriarch (see Gen. 14:13) from whom the nation of Israel ultimately descends, everyone is considered a Gentile, as opposed to in later times when only non-Hebrews/Israelites were designated as Gentiles (see Gal. 2:14–15). In this later sense, the Gentiles ("the nations") are distinguished from the original Israelites, with whom they are ultimately called to be one within the Church (see Eph. 2:11–16).

In the earlier usage of *Gentile*, Abram's forefathers, Abel and Noah, are listed as Gentiles too (CCC 58). Consequently, Melchizedek could also be an ancestor of Abram and still be described as a Gentile. A traditional argument made in ancient Jewish writings, and by the early Church Father St. Ephraem the Syrian, is that Shem, the righteous firstborn son of Noah, is Melchizedek.[21] (The words *Semite* and *Semitic* are derived from *Shem* or *Shemites*, illustrating that modern, ethnic Jews are descendants of Shem.) According to this argument, Shem received a blessing from Noah (Gen. 9:26) and eventually passed it on to his descendant Abraham (Gen. 14:18).

Scholars debate whether Abram's genealogy in Genesis 11 is exhaustive or just mentions certain figures among a longer list of ancestors. The Bible records that Shem lived 600 years (Gen.

[21] See, for example, Fr. James Meagher, *How Christ Said the First Mass* (New York: Christian Press Association Publishing, 1906), 219; see also 217–225. Reprinted by TAN Books and Publishers, Rockford, IL. See also Andrei A. Orlov's paper, "Noah's Younger Brother: The Anti-Noachic Polemics in 2 Enoch," at http://www.marquette.edu/maqom/noah.html. Orlov lists several ancient Jewish writings in his paper. Writing in the fourth century, St. Ephraem the Syrian affirmed Shem as Melchizedek in his *Commentary on Genesis* (sect. 11, 2, 4). Later that century, the Church Father St. Jerome recognized without dispute the "Shem as Melchizedek" view both in his *Hebrew Questions on Genesis*, specifically Gen. 14:18–19, and also in his Letter 73.5 on Melchizedek to the presbyter Evangelus. For more on the "Shem as Melchizedek" view, see the article by M. McNamara, M.S.C., "Melchizedek; Gen 14:17–20 in the Targums, in Rabbinic and Early Christian Literature," *Biblica 81* (2001), as given at http://www.bsw.org/biblica/vol-81-2000/melchizedek-gen-14-17-20-in-the-targums-in-rabbinic-and-early-christian-literature/276/.

11:10–11), while Abram only 175 (Gen. 25:7).[22] If the Bible's genealogical list of Abram's descendants were intended to be fairly exhaustive, a very elderly Shem could have walked the earth with Abram and blessed him, preceding him in death by only twenty-five years. But if the book of Genesis were written to provide only the highlights of Abram's ancestry in chapter 11, as many scholars believe,[23] Melchizedek would not have been Shem but perhaps one of his descendants, since the Bible never records that "the blessing" departed from Shem's line.

Other scholars believe that Melchizedek was a Canaanite priest-king or one of unknown genealogical origin. They argue that God could have raised up a priest outside of the Shemitic line and that, as a priest, this person could have provided a blessing irrespective of his ancestral pedigree.

Fact or Fiction?

Still other scholars and historians cast doubt on the historical reliability of Genesis in general, questioning whether Melchizedek and his priest-king "successor" David even existed. For years, these scholars have noted that there was no evidence outside the Bible for David's existence, let alone that of the much more ancient Melchizedek. The scriptural skeptics were shocked in 1993,

---

[22] Eugene H. Merrill, *Kingdom of Priests: A History of Old Testament Israel* (Grand Rapids, MI: Baker Books, 1997), 28.

[23] Ibid. Merrill argues that Shem's being a contemporary of Abram seems difficult to reconcile with the biblical data. Shem lived six hundred years, significantly fewer than his father Noah's 950, and yet Genesis 25:8 describes Abraham, who lived until age 175, as a man who "died in a good old age, an old man and full of years." In other words, the argument is that 575 must have been a *later* era's standard of old age and thus the much older Melchizedek could not have been a contemporary of Abraham.

though, when archaeologists discovered definitive extrabiblical evidence that King David reigned in Israel. They unearthed fragments from a ninth-century-B.C. monument recording that the king of Damascus had scored a victory over "the House of David," a reference to one of David's descendants. As Tel Aviv University archaeologist Israel Finkelstein noted, "Biblical nihilism collapsed overnight with the discovery of the David inscription."[24]

In addition, ancient Israel and the disciples of Jesus had no doubts about the historical reality of Melchizedek. David associated his royal heir with Melchizedek's priesthood. Psalm 110 speaks about how David's "lord," and therefore ultimately Jesus, is a priest forever "after the order of Melchizedek" (Ps. 110:1, 4). Because Solomon had ascended to the throne during his father David's lifetime (1 Kings 1:43) and thereby became the "lord king" (1 Kings 1:37), David could speak of his son as "my lord" (Ps. 110:1). As David's son and kingly lord, Solomon is the person whom God— that is, "*the* Lord"—first designated as a priest-king forever according to Melchizedek in some sense (Ps. 110:1, 4, emphasis added). David undoubtedly served as a priest-king (see 2 Sam. 6:12–13, 17; 24:25), as did Solomon (see 1 Kings 3:4, 5). As the ultimate "son of David" (Matt. 1:1), Jesus perfectly fulfills Psalm 110:4. In the New Covenant, Jesus is designated as a "high priest for ever after the order of Melchizedek" (Heb. 6:20), an order that fulfills the Levitical priesthood and laws that encompassed the various Old Covenant sacrifices that God prescribed (see Heb. 7:11–12).

---

[24] Jeffery L. Sheler, "Is the Bible True?: Extraordinary Insights from Archaeology and History," *US News and World Report*, October 25, 1999, 56; and 50–52. See also Dr. K. A. Kitchen's *On the Reliability of the Old Testament* (Grand Rapids, MI: Eerdmans, 2003).

What's Your Name? Who's Your Daddy?

To help identify Melchizedek, one must make sense of the strange description that the Letter to the Hebrews provides about the ancient priest-king.[25] Indeed, Melchizedek had an unusual priestly pedigree:

> For this Melchizedek, king of Salem, priest of the Most High God, met Abraham returning from the slaughter of the kings and blessed him; and to him Abraham apportioned a tenth part of everything. He is first, by translation of his name, king of righteousness, and then he is king of Salem, that is, king of peace. *He is without father or mother or genealogy, and has neither beginning of days nor end of life, but resembling the Son of God he continues a priest for ever.* (Heb. 7:1–3, emphasis added)

The mysterious words of Hebrews 7:3 have baffled many scholars, and we can appreciate why some have erroneously argued that Melchizedek was the Holy Spirit or the pre-Incarnate Word (see John 1:1–10,[26] since he "resembled the Son of God," was "without father or mother or genealogy," and had "neither beginning of days nor end of life."

Hebrews 7:1–3 becomes less mysterious when seen in light of the overall purpose of the whole chapter: to illustrate that Melchizedek's priesthood, particularly as fulfilled in Jesus, fulfills

---

[25] The idea of royal priesthood was not uncommon in the ancient Near Eastern world. See Merrill, *Kingdom of Priests*, 265.

[26] W. Leonard, D.S.S., "The Epistle to the Hebrews," in Dom Bernard Orchard et al., eds., *A Catholic Commentary on Holy Scripture* (New York: Thomas Nelson and Sons, 1953), 1165, no. 938e. See also Merrill, *Kingdom of Priests*, 264.

and supersedes the temporary Levitical law and priesthood (Heb. 7:11–14).

Comparing Priesthoods:
Levitical versus Melchizedekian

David came after Moses and Aaron in history, but he did not appeal to the Mosaic covenant and the Levitical priesthood to legitimize his kingdom. Rather, as Psalm 110 conveys, David links his royal line with the priest-kingship of Melchizedek. In addition, the Letter to the Hebrews notes that even Levi, one of the twelve tribes of Israel and therefore a descendant of Abraham and Isaac, recognized the superiority of Melchizedek. While Levitical priests beginning with Aaron received tithes from the Israelites (Num. 18:21–25), the superior nature of Melchizedek's priesthood is illustrated by Levi's "paying tithes" to the priest-king while still "in the loins" of Abraham the great patriarch (Heb. 7:9–10). In other words, when Abraham the great patriarch paid tithes to Melchizedek, he symbolically did so on behalf of all of his descendants, including Levi and his priestly descendants.

In addition, Levitical priestly service had a distinct "beginning of days and end of life" (see Heb. 7:3). Recall that God fulfilled his promise to make a great nation of Abram's descendants (Gen. 12) by establishing Israel via a covenant with Moses, who was of the tribe of Levi (Exod. 2:1–10). Under the Mosaic covenant, God chose the tribe of Levi not only to offer the sacrifices associated with the wilderness tabernacle (see Exod. 32:29) — and eventually those associated with the Temple — but also to be responsible for all of the tabernacle's furnishings (see Num. 1:47–54; 2:5–10). Those Levites who were direct descendants of Aaron were appointed priests (Exod. 40:12–15) and received assistance from their brother Levites (Num. 3:9–10). Any other Israelites who attempted to serve as priests would die (Num. 3:10; 18:7). In addition, all Levites, whether priests or not, had a distinct beginning and end of their service in the tabernacle and/or Temple, starting at age thirty and finishing at fifty (see, for example, Num. 4:1–3, 23).

Furthermore, all Levites who served in the wilderness tabernacle, and later the Temple, had to certify their genealogy, that is, furnish credible proof regarding the identity of their mother and father and other ancestors (see Heb. 7:3). We know this because, after the Babylonian Exile, when the Israelites returned to Jerusalem in the latter sixth century B.C., some alleged Levites were not allowed to serve in the rebuilt Temple, because "they could not prove their fathers' houses nor their descent" (Neh. 7:61; see 61–65; Ezra 2:59–63).

In contrast, Melchizedek possessed his priesthood not by virtue of his earthly mother or father, that is, his ancestral heritage, but because of a mysterious, special relationship with God. Whereas the sacrificial service of Levitical priests had "beginning of days" and "end of life," a limited ministry from ages thirty to fifty for which they had to be ordained, Melchizedek possessed his priesthood "for ever," that is, as a lifelong gift from God. Similarly, David's son King Solomon was "a priest for ever [according to] the order of Melchizedek" (Ps. 110:4), because his priesthood had no formal beginning or ending within his lifetime, even though he began to offer sacrifices only when he became king.

Jesus: Perfecting the Priesthood of Melchizedek

Jesus follows in the royal priestly "legacy" of Melchizedek and David (Matt. 1:1; 22:41–46), not Aaron's Levitical priesthood. He too is a "priest for ever according to the order of Melchizedek," yet in a profoundly different manner from Melchizedek and Solomon. Their priesthood ended with their deaths. Jesus manifested his Melchizedekian priesthood on earth in a distinctive way when he offered his life unto death. The Letter to the Hebrews summarizes: "Although he was a Son, he learned obedience through what he suffered; and being made perfect he became the source of eternal salvation to all who obey him, being designated as a high priest [according to] the order of Melchizedek" (Heb. 5:8–10).

How does Christ's Sacrifice continue forever, and how does he offer it according to the order of Melchizedek on earth? Suffice it to say for now that our Lord's Melchizedekian priesthood did not end with his death on Calvary; it was distinctively exercised on Calvary and continues forever. While Jesus offered himself "once for all" (Heb. 7:27), his one Sacrifice has an everlasting quality, for he "holds his priesthood *permanently*" and therefore "*always* lives to make intercession for us" (Heb. 7:24–25, emphasis added). How so? As will be discussed in detail in chapter 7, Jesus' Sacrifice was not completed with his death and Resurrection. After his Resurrection, Jesus told Mary Magdalene that he had not yet ascended to his Father (John 20:17). Only at the Ascension does Jesus enter the heavenly sanctuary and present his Father the glorified body, blood, soul, and divinity of his Self-Sacrifice (Heb. 9:23–24; see 9:12).

Because Jesus' Offering of Calvary enters into the time-transcendent heavenly sanctuary, it is an everlasting Offering and therefore continues forever. In addition, because his Sacrifice is not time-bound and thus continues forever, Jesus enables heaven and earth to intersect, empowering his Church on earth both to re-present and to partake of his Self-Offering under the sacramental forms of bread and wine, that is, according to the order of his Melchizedekian priesthood. The connections between Calvary and Christ's Melchizedekian priesthood will be explored more fully in chapter 2 of part 2 and chapter 3 of part 3.

Reverberating throughout Salvation History: Melchizedek's Blessing of Abram

Melchizedek's appearance is brief but powerful in Genesis. God chose Melchizedek to invoke a blessing on Abram, a blessing that would one day reverberate down to a descendant named Jesus (see Matt. 1:1), another priest-king. God told Abram that he would not only make of his descendants a great nation, but that he would also one day bless all nations through his descendants (see Gen. 12:1–3). Jesus would one day offer a Sacrifice for all mankind on Calvary, mysteriously pre-presenting and anticipating that Sacrifice at the Last Supper (CCC 1337; see CCC 1362–1367).

Other biblical evidence further links Melchizedek and Jesus. Melchizedek's name means "king of righteousness," while the prophesied Messiah was to come from the House of David and reign forever with justice and righteousness (see Isa. 9:6–7). Indeed, Jesus would fulfill the prophecy "the Lord is our righteousness" (Jer. 23:5–6).[27] In addition, Melchizedek reigns over Salem ("peace"), a location that David equates with "Zion" (Ps. 76:2), the kingdom city also identified as Jerusalem (Ps. 2:6; Isa. 24:23). One day in Jerusalem, the "Prince of Peace" (Isa. 9:6) would triumph on the Cross.

---

[27] The title is apparently and ironically first accorded to King Zedekiah, who became corrupt. See Rev. M. McNamara, M.S.C., "Jeremiah," in *A New Catholic Commentary on Holy Scripture,* revised and updated edition, Rev. Reginald C. Fuller, gen. ed. (Nashville: Thomas Nelson, 1975), 614, no. 495g.

Bread and Wine and without Beginning or End

Questions for Reflection or Group Discussion

1. (a) Why did Abram pay attention to Melchizedek? (b) Abram honored God and Melchizedek by paying "tithes," that is, the first 10 percent of his earnings. Do you tithe, or have you considered tithing? (c) How might the discipline of tithing help you to deal better with material and spiritual trials? (See Matt. 6:33 and Mal 3:10.)

2. (a) Who might Melchizedek be? (b) Why does Shem or one of his descendants seem to be a reasonable candidate? Explain. (c) What biblical evidence beyond Genesis attests to the historical reality of Melchizedek? (d) What nonbiblical evidence supports the historical reality of David?

3. (a) In light of the Letter to the Hebrews and other biblical evidence discussed, how should we understand that Melchizedek had no father or mother and was without beginning or end? In answering this question, explain how the Levitical priesthood was different from that of Melchizedek. (b) How does the Letter to the Hebrews argue that the Levitical priesthood is inferior to that of Melchizedek?

4. (a) How does Melchizedek's sacrifice prefigure Christ's Sacrifice? (b) Considering the material discussed in this chapter, what other biblical evidence links Melchizedek, Jesus Christ, and the latter's ultimate blessing for the whole world?

5. (a) How is Jesus' priesthood similar to and different from that of Melchizedek and Solomon? (b) What preliminary biblical evidence can you provide that Christ's priesthood and Self-Offering continue beyond his death and Resurrection, that his Offering is "once for all," yet everlasting?

5

Emancipation Proclamation
Abraham Receives God's Saving Word

Background Reading
   Genesis 12:1–3
   Genesis 15–1
   Genesis 21:1–21
   Genesis 22:1–18

Jesus teaches us that salvation — that is, emancipation from sin and death — comes from the Jews (John 4:22). To appreciate what Jesus is saying, we have to understand his New Testament words in light of their Old Testament heritage. The word *Jew* refers to a member of the tribe of Judah, one of the twelve tribes of Jacob, the patriarch who was later renamed Israel (Gen. 35:10). (Judah's most prominent descendants were David, Jesus, and Jesus' mother, Mary). Jacob's father was Isaac, whose father, in turn, was the great patriarch Abraham. Abraham himself was a Hebrew (Gen. 14:13), a name that appears to have derived from his ancestor Eber (see Gen. 11:14). Eber, in turn, descended from Shem (Gen. 10:21), the son whom Noah blessed (Gen. 9:26).

Genesis 12:1–3 has been called "the acorn of salvation history," because God promised Abram, as Abraham was first known, that he would make a great nation of his descendants, who would ultimately be a blessing to all nations. God fleshes out his plan in Genesis 15, 17, and 22, swearing covenant oaths to Abram that he will make of his descendants:

- a great nation (chap. 15), fulfilled in the Hebrews' liberation from Egyptian enslavement and their formation as the nation of Israel

- a kingdom (chap. 17), fulfilled in the kingdom of Israel that began with King David and continued with his descendants

- a blessing to all the nations (chap. 22), fulfilled in his descendant Jesus (Matt. 1:1), who offers to the whole world emancipation from sin and death.

From the beginning of salvation history, we see that God mediates his covenants through *visible, human* structures, appointing human authorities to govern his people in his name. We are also reminded that his plan will ultimately bring about a universal, or "catholic," blessing, because it will encompass all the nations. In addition, whereas a contract is typically a temporary exchange of services, an authentic covenant creates unbreakable relationships between persons that have solemn obligations. If a contract is broken, its terms can be fulfilled in ways other than rendering the contracted services; for example, through providing financial compensation.[28] Because a covenant

---

[28] A notable exception is the sacrament of Marriage, which is both a contract and a covenant and thus indissoluble.

is by nature unbreakable, it cannot be negotiated away through alternative compensation. Instead, the relationship must be restored. Therefore, while covenant violations invariably invoke curses, these curses are designed to remedy or restore the right relationship of the covenant parties.

By examining the biblical text and ancient Near Eastern covenants, one is able to conclude that God is swearing covenant oaths in Genesis 15, 17, and 22. Yet, while other peoples of the ancient Near East invoked God as a *witness* to their solemn oaths, only with Israel did God become an actual *covenant partner* and swear oaths himself. That is, only with Israel did God swear that he would be willing to suffer, that is, suffer a remedial curse, for a violation of a covenant.

I'm Willing to Die for This

The gravity of an oath is illustrated in Genesis 15. God passes between sacrificed animal parts, indicating that he would rather be split in two (15:17–18) than not fulfill his commitment to make Abram's descendants a great nation.[29] Although God would never break a promise, his swearing elevates his promise to a covenant oath, and his passing through the animal parts in a solemn ritual enacts or seals his covenant oath. God also foretells the Hebrews' extended Egyptian bondage but makes a covenant oath that they will eventually gain freedom and a vast area of land (15:14, 18–21).

---

[29] See Scott Hahn, *A Father Who Keeps His Promises: God's Covenant Law in Scripture* (Ann Arbor, MI: Servant Publications, 1998), 100–101. God's willingness to die for Abram seems to be an early foreshadowing of the Cross. Abram would suffer the same penalty if he did not fulfill his oath to be faithful to God. Jeremiah 34:18–20 affirms the gravity of such a solemn, sacrificial ritual.

In Genesis 17, Abram ("exalted") is renamed "Abraham" ("father of a multitude") because he will become "the father of a multitude of nations" (17:5). God tells Abraham that kings will come forth from him, foretelling the kingdom of David, with whom he would establish an everlasting covenant (Gen. 17:6–7; see 2 Sam. 7:12–19). When we examine more closely God's covenant ratification with David in 2 Samuel, we discover that God will use the kingdom of Israel to provide a *"Torah for adam,"* that is, a "law for man" (see note on 2 Sam 7:19 in the Revised Standard Version Catholic Edition [RSVCE]). This passage indicates that God's ultimate blessing for all nations will somehow come through the Davidic kingdom of Israel.

Has Anybody Seen My Firstborn, Isaac?

But who will carry on the covenant? Melchizedek blessed Abraham, but whom will Abraham bless? Ishmael, whom Abraham fathered through his wife's maidservant Hagar, might have appeared the early favorite because he was the first child that the great patriarch fathered. But God had other ideas, as will become apparent. In Genesis 15, God brought Abram (as he was then still named) outside and asked him to count the stars of the sky, if he were able. As numerous as the stars are, God told Abram, so too "shall your descendants be" (Gen. 15:5). Abram believed, and God credited it to him as righteousness (Gen. 15:5–7).

Nevertheless, Abram quickly experienced difficulties in his walk of faith. He did not categorically reject God, but he tried to carry out God's plan through his own efforts, apparently assuming that the Lord would bless his adaptations. After God made his first covenant with Abram, the patriarch and his wife, Sarai, grew tired of waiting for Sarai to bear children. Consequently, Abram and his wife decided that the blessing would come through the offspring of Sarai's maidservant Hagar (Gen. 16). We learn that this improvisation was not God's will (see Gen. 2:23–24), because he promised Sarai — whom he renamed Sarah[30] — that she would bear a son, Isaac, with whom he would establish his covenant (17:15–21). The renamed Abraham initially thought God's idea laughable (17:17), as did Sarah (18:9–16), given their advanced age. But the Lord revealed to Abraham and Sarah, as he would later reveal to Elizabeth's husband, Zechariah (Luke 1:5–21), that nothing is impossible for him, including overcoming an elderly woman's barrenness.

Prefiguring Calvary: Abraham Offers Up Isaac

As divinely foretold, Sarah bore a son, and God told Abraham that "through Isaac shall your descendants be named" (Gen. 21:12). A short while later, God told Abraham, "Take your son, your only son Isaac, whom you love, and go to the land of Moriah and offer him there as a burnt offering upon one of the mountains of which I shall tell you" (Gen. 22:2). That is a divine word that must have given Abraham great pause: "Only son? The land of Moriah? And offer as a burnt sacrifice the son through whom God is supposed to fulfill all of his covenants with me?"

Scripture scholars have also greatly pondered what we might term Genesis 22:2's scriptural "speed bump." Let us consider each issue in turn. We know that Abraham fathered two sons, but only one was an heir to the covenant[31] God established with the patriarch:

---

[30] *Sarah* means "princess" or "queen."

[31] We can speak collectively of the three covenants God made with Abraham as "the covenant."

As for Ishmael, I have heard you; behold, I will bless him and make him fruitful and multiply him exceedingly; he shall be the father of twelve princes, and I will make him a great nation. But I will establish my covenant with Isaac, whom Sarah shall bear to you at this season next year. (Gen. 17:20–21)

Note that our father in faith received the name Abraham in anticipation of Isaac's birth, not in relation to his fathering of Ishmael. God would take care of Hagar and Ishmael (Gen. 21:14–21), but, according to God's saving plan, Isaac was "the man." Ishmael was born according to *Abraham's* attempt to improvise God's plan. Isaac was born according to *God's* provision for the elderly patriarch, the Almighty letting Abraham know early on that he was fully capable of providing all of his sworn blessings.

Abraham's faith in God's providence, though, was being tested again in Genesis 22. The choice of Moriah must have caused turmoil for Abraham. Recall from the previous chapter that *Salem* was synonymous with *Zion* (Ps. 76:2) and *Zion* with *Jerusalem*, the central city of God's Kingdom that would be founded later in salvation history (Ps. 2:6; Isa. 24:23). While God indicated he would direct Abraham to a specific mountain (Gen. 22:2), the book of Genesis seems to imply that Abraham knew about Moriah, because there is no further explanation by God or question by Abraham about the proposed sacrificial site. Considering other biblical evidence, we can reasonably conclude that Abraham knew that the mountains of Moriah encompassed Salem, later known as Jerusalem (see 2 Chron. 3:1). God was asking Abraham to go to the land of Melchizedek, the priest-king who had blessed him after his battlefield conquests (see

Gen. 14:4–20). But sacrificing Isaac did not sound like a cause for celebration. How could the nations be blessed through Isaac's descendants if Isaac himself were killed before he bore any children? Despite the meaning of its name, Salem probably did not seem very "peaceful" to Abraham at this point.

Abraham, his two servants, and Isaac traveled on, gathering wood along the way. On the third day—a day to which Jesus also gave great significance via his own Sacrifice—Abraham saw the mountainous place of sacrifice in the distance. Father and son continued on alone, Isaac carrying the heavy wood while his father brought the knife and the fire. The unsuspecting Isaac asked the inevitable question: "Behold, the fire and the wood; but where is the lamb for a burnt offering?" Abraham responded, "God will provide himself the lamb for a burnt offering, my son" (Gen. 22:7–8).

Finally, the pair arrived at Moriah. After preparing the wood, Abraham bound Isaac, laid him on the altar of sacrifice and, obedient to God's command, raised the knife to kill his son. But the angel of the Lord stopped Abraham from carrying out the sacrifice, commending his fidelity to God, because "you have not withheld your son, your only son, from me" (Gen. 22:12).

Like Fathers, Like Sons

Still, God's command puzzles us. Why would God command Abraham to sacrifice his *only* son, when he had promised to fulfill his covenants through that same son? Yet Abraham had confidence that God would, if necessary, resurrect Isaac to fulfill his covenant oaths (see Heb. 11:17–19). Looking ahead in the biblical story of the Mass for a moment, we can see that the Father did not ask of Abraham something he would not ask of himself or his own Son, Jesus. Abraham and Isaac would prefigure the infinite, eternal love of Father and Son. Jesus, the most important descendant of Abraham and Isaac, would actually lay down his life and even appear defeated for a few days.

Abraham substituted a ram for Isaac and named the mountain "the Lord will provide" (Gen. 22:14), the Hebrew words for which are *Yahweh yireh*. Some scholars believe that the Jews may have eventually combined *Yahweh yireh* (or *Jireh*) and the city's older name (Salem) to form *Jireh-Salem*, or Jerusalem ("he [Yaweh] will provide peace").[32]

How strange that Abraham names the mountain "the Lord will provide" after God provided a ram that, if young enough, could have been classified as a lamb. Abraham told Isaac that God "will provide" the lamb and yet, after the Lord provided a ram to sacrifice instead of Abraham's son, Abraham still named the mountain "the Lord will provide," not "the Lord did provide." In the very next line, the book of Genesis adds with apparent emphasis, "[A]s it is said to this day, 'On the mount of the Lord it shall be provided'" (Gen. 22:14; emphasis added), clearly conveying an expectation that God would one day yet provide a lamb.

Because of Abraham's fidelity, God swore one final oath with the patriarch, first reaffirming that his descendants would be numerous and conquer their enemies. God then elevated his final promise from Genesis 12:3 to covenant-oath status: "[B]y your descendants shall all the nations of the earth bless themselves, because you have obeyed my voice" (Gen. 22:18; see 22:15–18).

The Jews refer to this story as the *Aqedah*,[33] Hebrew for "binding." And while we initially ponder Abraham's binding of Isaac,

---

[32] Tim Gray, "Where Is the Lamb for the Sacrifice?" *Lay Witness*, March 1997, 4–5.

[33] Also spelled Akedah.

we can also see that God bound himself to Abraham, his descendants, and ultimately the world, swearing an oath that he would fulfill his final promise to Abraham to bless all the nations. God linked the fulfillment of this universal blessing with a lamb that he would somehow provide on Mount Moriah / Zion in Jerusalem. Abraham could not actually see another sacrifice that far into the future on this same Jerusalem mount, but his faith allowed him to envision its fulfillment.

While God credited Abraham's faith, the event became known among ancient Jews as the "sacrifice of Isaac." The ancient rabbis believed that Isaac was somewhere between eighteen and thirty-seven years old when he was offered up on Mount Moriah.[34] As an adult, Isaac would have presumably been able to resist his elderly father had he wanted, for Abraham was ninety-nine when his son was conceived (Gen. 17:1). Some ancient Jewish commentaries argue that Isaac willingly submitted to his father and ultimately to God, and that is why ancient Jews also described the Aqedah as the sacrifice of Isaac.[35] (Here we see that sacrifice is defined, not by blood, but by the will. Men can make a self-offering to God without shedding their blood, although, in this case, Isaac was willing to die. In general, and in the case of Isaac, human sacrifice is made by another type of death — death

---

[34] Robert Hayward, "The Present State of Research into the Targumic Account of the Sacrifice of Isaac," *Journal of Jewish Studies* 32 (August 1981): 132. For example, writing in the first century, Josephus says that Isaac was twenty-five (*Antiquities* 1.227).

[35] Hayward, "The Present State of Research into the Targumic Account of the Sacrifice of Isaac," 130, 135. In addition, writing to the Corinthians in the first century, Pope Clement I affirms that Isaac "cheerfully yielded himself as a sacrifice" (First Clement, 31), as cited in Alexander Roberts and James Donaldson, *Ante-Nicene Fathers* (Peabody, MA: Hendrickson Publishers, 1994), 1:13.

to oneself by complete and obedient surrender to God's will.) A couple of thousand years later on the same mountain, another descendant of Abraham — the Lamb of God that the Father would provide — would perfect the model of obedient Sonship.[36]

Questions for Reflection and Discussion

1. (a) What is a covenant? (b) What is the basic difference between a covenant and a contract? (c) What happens to one who violates a covenant? (d) What are the three covenants God made with Abraham? Or, said another way, what are the three phases of the covenant God made with Abraham?

2. In Genesis 15, God tested Abram's faith, telling him that his descendants would be as numerous as the stars of the sky. (a) How might we relate Abram's test to our faith in the Eucharist and the Sacrifice of the Mass? (Hint: faith must supply what our senses cannot perceive.) (b) How could the apostle Thomas (see John 20:24–29) have applied the lesson of Abram in his life, and how can we do so today in our own lives?

3. Abram and Sarai were not always faithful to God, as exemplified by their attempt to fulfill God's covenant through Hagar and Ishmael, the son Hagar bore with Abram. (a) God conveyed to Abraham that Isaac was his "only" son. What was God trying

---

[36] Following the healing of a lame man, Peter teaches a Jewish crowd that Genesis 22:18 has its fulfillment in Christ, the heavenly Father's only Son: "You are the sons of the prophets and of the covenant which God gave to your fathers, saying to Abraham, 'And in your posterity shall all the families of the earth be blessed.' God, having raised up his servant, sent him to you first, to bless you in turning every one of you from your wickedness" (Acts 3:25–26).

to tell Abraham and his wife? (b) Have there been times when you asked God to bless your plans or assumed he would do so, whether regarding a relationship, a work matter, or something else? (c) What did you learn from these experiences?

4. Abraham and Sarah laughed at God's promise that Sarah, a woman well past childbearing years, would conceive a son. The name of the child that they eventually had, Isaac, means "laughter," and indicates that God had the last laugh. (a) Have you laughed at God's ability to provide for you, only to be humbly, yet happily, surprised at his providence? (b) Can you think of any New Testament stories that parallel the account of Abraham and Sarah's expecting an unexpected child? (c) In Luke 1, compare and contrast the respective responses of Zechariah and the Virgin Mary to God's promise of a "miracle baby."

5. Compare what God asked of Abraham with what God asked of himself. (a) Did God ask more of Abraham regarding Isaac than he was willing to sacrifice regarding his own Son? In answering, consider that God asked Abraham to "bind" Isaac to the altar but then concluded by "binding" himself to Abraham and his descendants. (b) Given Isaac's youth and his father's advanced age at the time of his offering, some Jewish traditions shifted the focus away from Abraham's faithfulness to Isaac's willingness. Why is this significant? (c) Based on the information we learned about Salem and Moriah from this chapter and the previous one, what might we expect to occur there and why, as the biblical story of the Mass unfolds? (Hint: In what way or ways does Isaac prefigure Jesus?)

Part 2

Prefiguring the Mass
in the Old Covenant

6

From Moriah to the Messiah
Understanding How God Provides
the Lamb through the Passover

Background Reading
   Exodus 3:1-22; 8:25–32; 12
   Genesis 22
   Luke 22

The next major step God took toward establishing the sacrificial meal of the Mass occurred with the Exodus. God foretold that Abraham's descendants would become slaves "in a land that is not theirs and they will be oppressed four hundred years" (Gen. 15:13). That land was Egypt, and his descendants became known as "Israel" (see Exod. 2:23–25). In renaming Jacob (Abraham's grandson) Israel, God swore that "a nation and company of nations shall come from you, and kings shall spring from you" (Gen. 35:10–11), reaffirming the covenants he had made with Abraham (see Gen. 15 and 17). "The land which I gave to Abraham and Isaac I will give to you," God told Jacob, "and I will give the land to your descendants after you" (Gen. 35:12).

Moses became the descendant who would deliver Israel from Egyptian bondage (Exod. 3:1–22; see Gen. 15:14), a deliverance popularized in the Hollywood film epic *The Ten Commandments*. Moses told Pharaoh to let Israel go, so that God's people could celebrate a sacrificial feast in his honor in the wilderness (Exod. 5:3). The Israelites would have to offer sacrifice outside of Egypt, because God intended to wean his people from four hundred years of idolatry in a radical way: having them sacrifice the animals they were tempted to worship—that is, those that represented Egyptian gods, including bulls. Moses knew such sacrifices would provoke the wrath of the Egyptians, so he pleaded with Pharaoh for Israel's release (Exod. 8:25–27).[37] Having endured several plagues, Pharaoh relented temporarily, but then again refused to let Israel go (Exod. 8:28–32).

---

[37] While many modern scholars do not believe that God instituted animal sacrifices to wean his people from attachment to Egyptian idols, that is, by slaying the gods they once worshipped in offering righteous worship to him, there is considerable support for this reading of Exodus 8:25–27. It is affirmed in Egyptian (Manetho quoted in Josephus, *Against Apion* 1, 26), Jewish (Moses Maimonides, *Guide for the Perplexed* 3, 46), and Roman antiquity (Tacitus, *Histories* 5, 4). The view is also affirmed by various early Church Fathers, including St. Justin Martyr, *Dialogue with Trypho* 19 and 22; St. Irenaeus, *Against Heresies* 3, 15; Eusebius, *Demonstration of the Gospel* 1, 4; St. Athanasius, *Letters* 19, 4; St. John Chrysostom, *Discourses against Judaizing Christians* 4, 6, 5; and St. Aphrahat, *Demonstrations* 15, 4 and 15, 6. It is also affirmed in the *Constitutions of the Holy Apostles* 6, 4, 20. For further reading on this subject, see Stephen D. Benin, *The Footprints of God: Divine Accommodation in Jewish and Christian Thought* (Albany, NY: State University of New York Press, 1993), particularly 2–10, 13–30, 40–41, 76–80.

Finally, after enduring three days of darkness, the ninth plague, Pharaoh told Moses never to show his face before him again, lest he die (Exod. 10:28). Pharaoh's ultimatum elicited one final plague: a divinely delivered death sentence for all of Egypt's firstborn men and livestock (Exod. 11:1–6). But the Lord had an insurance plan for Israel: the providing of sacrificial lambs. Wherever God saw an Israelite home marked with the blood of a lamb on its doorposts and lintel, he would "pass over," sparing the household's firstborn from the final plague that descended on Egypt (Exod. 12:12–13). The final plague gained Israel its independence, as Pharaoh finally relented and let God's people go.

Anticipating the Mass, the Passover featured not simply the sacrifice of lambs but also their consumption. The lambs had to be unblemished in physical constitution and appearance (Exod. 12:5), prefiguring Christ, who was unblemished by sin. God also told the Israelites not to break any of the lambs' bones (Exod. 12:46), a Passover prescription the Romans would also unknowingly maintain by not breaking Jesus' legs when he was on the Cross (John 19:36).

"Forever" Yours:
The Passover Sacrifice, Isaac, and the Messiah

The Passover event had another distinctive feature. While the shedding of lambs' blood and the Exodus were most notable that first Passover night, another event with great significance in salvation history quietly took place earlier that month: God instituted the Passover sacrifice as an "ordinance for ever" (Exod. 12:14, 17, 24), that is, a perpetual ordinance. As used in the Bible, though, *for ever* does not necessarily mean for all earthly time, let alone for all eternity. *For ever* can mean for an entire period of salvation history, but only for that period, such as with Solomon's Temple and its replacement, which were intended by God to serve for only a limited time in salvation history on earth. Their collective purpose was effectively served when Jesus died, rose from the dead and ascended into heaven, even though the latter Temple stood until A.D. 70 (see 1 Kings 8:13; Matt. 27:51; 24:1–2). *For ever* can also mean that an ordinance might endure a salvation history transition, yet be transformed and celebrated in a fulfilled manner, such as in a "new covenant." Suffice it to say for now that the Passover would not be a one-time event, a simple memory. The sacrifice would continue year after year. God designed the Passover to be both a memory and a meal, a past event and yet a perpetual celebration, and, as we will see, a template that would prefigure the Eucharistic liturgy of the New Covenant. Recall too that God, after Abraham offered Isaac on Mount Moriah, swore a covenant oath to the patriarch that he would one day provide "the lamb" on that mount, a lamb that would bring a blessing to all the nations (Gen. 22:14, 18). While the Passover celebration initially took place in Egypt and involved many lambs versus a single one, the possibility existed that Passover and the universal blessing could one day overlap.

In fact, ancient Jewish writings called Targums establish a link between the Passover and the sacrifice of Isaac. In Jesus' day, Targums were used in the synagogues with the Scriptures of Israel. Targums are free translations of scriptural passages mixed with commentary and homiletic material. Their authors paraphrased and interpreted Scripture, making the Old Testament accessible to Jews who spoke Aramaic, the language that replaced Hebrew as the common language of the ancient Jews. For our purposes, Targums are important because they throw light on the Passover as it was understood in Jewish antiquity, educating the masses about the intimate connections between the ancient sacrifice of Isaac on Moriah and that of the subsequent Passover. Sacrificial lambs helped liberate both Isaac and Israel, a ram standing in for Isaac on Moriah and a host of lambs aiding Israel's deliverance from centuries-long bondage in Egypt. As noted in the last chapter, Isaac's sacrifice was known as the Aqedah—a Hebrew designation to denote Abraham's "binding" of Isaac—but a greater tie bound Isaac and the Passover. Isaac's sacrifice—his willingness to die for his father and God—anticipated a greater lamb offering on Moriah, one that would liberate not simply a nation but *all* nations (see Gen. 22: 18). In fact, ancient Jews believed that Isaac's sacrifice had an enduring significance: that it overshadowed and gave meaning to the first and subsequent Passover sacrifices. The Targums leave no doubt about the connection the Jews saw between the Passover and the Aqedah: "And when I see the blood [of the Passover lamb], I will pass over you (Ex 12:13)—I see the blood of Isaac's Aqedah."[38]

The "Poem of the Four Nights," which is contained in *Targum Neofiti,* expounds on the Passover legislation of Exodus 12. The poem explicitly links Isaac's sacrifice in Genesis 22 (the Aqedah) with God's oath in Genesis 15 that he would deliver Abraham's descendants from a future bondage in Egypt. The four nights were, respectively, (1) creation, (2) Isaac's birth and offering at the Aqedah, (3) the Exodus, and (4) the Messianic redemption

---

[38] *Mekhilta de Rabbi Ishmael,* Pisha 7, lines 78–79, as cited in Robert Hayward, "The Present State of Research," 140. The *Mekhilta de Rabbi Ishmael* is part of the Jewish Midrash, which is composed of rabbinical commentaries and explanatory notes on the Scriptures. These commentaries and notes were written between the beginning of the Babylonian Exile (587 B.C.) and circa A.D. 1200. The *Mekhilta* was written in the early Christian centuries.

of Israel.[39] The poem says that both the Aqedah and Passover took place on what would become known as Passover night.[40] The ancient Jews saw Passover as an initial, national fulfillment of Isaac's sacrifice that would one day culminate in a universal redemption. The Passover lambs prefigured a greater lamb, the one God swore to deliver on Moriah. For one day, on the evening of Passover, the Messiah, God's "anointed" lamb, would arrive to deliver Israel and the whole world:

> The Fourth Night, *when the world will reach its end to be redeemed.*... This is the night of the Passover to the Name of the Lord; it is a night reserved and appointed for redemption for all Israel, for their generations.[41]

The ancient Jews clearly drew a distinction between the redemption from Egyptian bondage that was limited to Israel in the first Passover and the worldwide redemption that the Messiah

---

[39] Hayward, "The Present State of Research into the Targumic Account of the Sacrifice of Isaac," 140.

[40] Ibid., 127. Hayward notes that some scholars maintain that the basic elements of the Aqedah can be discerned in Jewish writings of the first century B.C. and the first century A.D. and could thus have influenced New Testament authors in writing about Jesus' redemptive Sacrifice; yet he adds that others argue that it was invented by rabbinical authorities in the second century A.D. as a Jewish counterpoint to the Christian doctrine of Christ's atoning Sacrifice. Hayward illustrates that the most persuasive evidence is for an earlier dating of the targumic Aqedah's origins.

[41] *Targum Neofiti* to Exodus 12:42, as cited in *The Aramaic Bible, vol. 2—Targum Neofiti 1: Exodus*, translated with introduction and apparatus by Martin McNamara, M.S.C., and notes by Robert Hayward; *Targum Pseudo Jonathan: Exodus*, translated with notes by Michael Maher, M.S.C. (Collegeville, MN: Liturgical Press, 1994),52–53, emphasis added.

would ultimately deliver.[42] In addition, neither the Old Testament nor the Targums ever note that the Passover sacrifice would ever end, even with the arrival of the Messiah. God tells Moses *three times* that he and his descendants are to keep the Passover as an "ordinance for ever" (Exod. 12:14, 17, 24). Again, *for ever* can mean only as long as a covenant's particular prescriptions are in effect, but, as noted above, God could maintain and yet adapt a perpetual provision in a new covenant that fulfilled an old one.

In fact, as we will examine in more detail in subsequent chapters, this is precisely what Jesus did. At the Last Supper, at which Jesus explicitly celebrated the Passover (see Luke 22:15), the evangelists make no mention of a lamb. One would expect a traditional Passover lamb to be eaten, but one is not mentioned. The focus of Passover had clearly shifted to Jesus. In a dramatic transformation of the Passover rite — according to a New Covenant, which was prophesied by Jeremiah (see Jer. 31:31–33; Luke 22:20) — Jesus would offer himself as "the Lamb of God, who takes away the sin of the world" (John 1:29; see Luke 22:37; Matt. 26:28), perfecting Isaac's Aqedah. Jesus would be the Lamb that the Father would finally provide. Like Abraham with Isaac on Mount Moriah (see Gen. 2:16), our heavenly Father would "not spare his own Son but [would give] him up for us all" (Rom. 8:34).

Questions for Reflection and Discussion

1. Consider the feast of Passover. (a) How did the lamb sacrificed become known as the Passover or paschal lamb? (b) Provide a scriptural example of how the Passover lamb prefigured Christ.

[42] In time, Israel would learn that this later redemption would not simply be larger in scope — worldwide — but in significance, bringing emancipation from sin, not simply human bondage.

2. God provided that Passover would be an "ordinance for ever," indicating that its celebration could overlap with the fulfillment of the Aqedah. (a) What evidence, scriptural and otherwise—for example, the "Poem of the Four Nights"—connects Passover with the fulfillment of the Aqedah? (b) Did serving as an ordinance forever preclude the Passover from being modified? Explain.

7

Thanks for the "Memories"
The Passover Sacrifice, Then and Now

Background Reading
    Exodus 3:1–22; 8:25–32; 12
    Genesis 22
    Luke 22
    Hebrews 7–9
    Leviticus 1:3–10; 16:11–15
    Revelation 5:1–14
    Catechism of the Catholic Church, nos. 645–646, 659, 1085

Before its New Covenant transformation at the Last Supper, the Passover ordinance would have to be celebrated as a "memorial" or "remembrance" each year of the Old Covenant. The annual celebration of the Passover, however, was not simply a memory for the Israelites, as the annual ritual of Independence Day is for Americans. In the United States, we draw inspiration from Independence Day when commemorating it each year on July 4. We may even restage the signing of the Declaration of Independence. Or we may commemorate it and the subsequent Revolutionary War otherwise, such as in parades or other festivities.

But the July 4, 1776, event does not possess any enduring power in itself. It remains a timebound historical event that we merely recall, although we do so in celebrating our current freedoms as Americans.

Similarly, the Israelites would recall the Passover event in their minds, becoming conscious again of how God had freed them (or their ancestors) from the bondage of Egypt. They would also consider the Passover's importance for them in the present. Yet, the Israelites did more than simply recall the highlights of the first Passover so that its liberating lessons would not be forgotten. For the Israelites, *remembering* was never simply a commemoration of a past event; it had a much more powerful meaning. Memory and action are intrinsically connected in the Bible, for to remember a past event is to *call forth the power of that past event and feel its impact in the present*. It is to *be* there, to relive the actual event in some sense (see CCC 1363). To convey *remembrance* in this special, biblical way, the Israelites would use the Hebrew verb *zakar* and its cognates.

The original Passover, though, would always remain a limited past event in *terms of its human and animal participants*. Moses, Pharaoh, and the others lived out the Passover in a specific time and place; their original actions began and ended that day, and new lambs would have to be sacrificed in subsequent years.

So how could Israel bring about such a remembrance? By invoking the power of its God. Because God himself was an intimate participant in the first Passover, biblical remembrance becomes decisively different from the mere human remembrance associated with Independence Day and similar events. When the Israelites remembered the Passover, God enabled the original event to transcend time somehow and impact the present. His action that first Passover possessed an enduring power that the Israelites could tap into again and again every time they celebrated the feast. For God, such remembrance is not difficult because he is the all-powerful Creator and Lord of time. He acts within time but, as the eternal God, he also transcends all time. All time is present to him, and therefore he is not limited or boxed in by time. He is superhistorical, for he stands outside of or above time, which enables him to be present to and impact *all* time, all human history. That means God's choices can reverberate throughout time as he wills. A British biblical scholar explains how this remembering impacts salvation history:

> Adam's original status before God is restored in Abraham and Isaac by their obedience to God's will,[43] and their descendants are to share in that restoration, since Israel, son of Isaac, is a Unique people. It is the *Aqedah* which bestows this uniqueness, through sacrifice offered on the altar *in Jerusalem. Future sacrifices "recall" the Aqedah and take their meaning from it; they, too, are designed to restore broken relationships between God and the offerers.*[44]

In short, God's is the gift that truly keeps on giving; he simply has to remember a covenant promise to bring his blessing to bear on the present moment.[45]

In commanding that the Passover be a "memorial," that is, an "ordinance for ever" (Exod. 12:14), God invited successive

---

[43] This point is certainly overstated, because only in Christ can mankind be restored to and elevated beyond Adam's original status before God (see CCC 412).

[44] Robert Hayward, "The Present State of Research into the Targumic Account of the Sacrifice of Isaac," 139, emphasis added.

[45] Léon-Dufour, *Sharing the Eucharistic Bread*, 102.

generations of Israelites to acknowledge and draw upon the divine power of the original event. In the process, Israel would realize that the Passover was not simply directed to Moses and the Israelites at the time of the Exodus, but rather was a transhistorical event in which God saw all of Israel's descendants. Thus, while the Israelites sacrificed new lambs each year to reexperience the Passover, past and present were always bridged with the remembrance of the inaugural offering, a remembrance that invoked anew, in the present, God's enduring blessing. Later generations did not miss this crucial aspect of the Passover-Exodus story, and that is why the Jewish Mishnah, the part of the Talmud[46] containing oral laws based on the Pentateuch, can say, "In celebrating the feast, we must act as though we ourselves had come up from Egypt" (Pesahim 10, 5).[47]

He Died Once, but His Sacrifice Lives On

How do we "remember" Christ's Sacrifice in the New Covenant Passover? The Church teaches that the Mass miraculously represents Christ's *one* Sacrifice under the appearances of bread and wine, and yet we know that Jesus died only once. How can we reconcile these two realities, which apparently conflict?

---

[46] The Talmud was divided into two parts: the Mishnah, whose oral laws were composed of rabbinic sayings and traditions compiled in the third century A.D., and the Gemarah, which provides commentary on the Mishnah. There is the Palestinian Gemarah and the Babylonian Gemarah, the latter completed in the sixth century. The Babylonian Gemarah is the longer version and also the more accepted among Jews. The Pentateuch, or Torah, consists of the first five books of the Old Testament and contains the written or scriptural law for Jews.

[47] As cited in Léon-Dufour, *Sharing the Eucharistic Bread*, 106.

The answer lies in understanding how sacrifices are offered to God in general and how Jesus offered his Sacrifice in particular. In the Old Testament, there were several types of sacrifice. Those that involved the slaughter of a live victim shared two distinct, yet interdependent phases. That is, you could not have an authentic sacrifice without completing both phases. First, a lay worshipper would usually *sacrifice* a victim—that is, begin the process of delivering over a victim to God by slaughtering it. Second, a priest, who served as God's designated mediator for the people, would *offer* the sacrifice, making contact with God and mediating relations with him on behalf of the people through the offering of the sacrificial victim. For example, the priest would apply the victim's blood to the altar, which represented God, or he would send the sacrificial aroma of a victim's burnt body heavenward as "a pleasing odor" to God (see Lev. 1:3–10).

To explain the twofold phases of biblical sacrifices that involved the slaughter of victims, let us consider the sacrifices offered on the Day of Atonement (Yom Kippur). Along with the Passover offering of lambs, the Day of Atonement sacrifices were the most important offerings of the Old Covenant that God made with Moses. As the Letter to the Hebrews teaches, the Day of Atonement sacrifices both prefigured and were perfected by Christ's once-for-all Sacrifice of himself.

Once a year on the Day of Atonement, as described in Leviticus 16:1–34, the high priest of Israel would sacrifice a bull and two goats to atone for his sins and those of the nation, respectively![48] To do so, he would enter the wilderness

---

[48] There were other offerings this day, as noted in Leviticus 16, but only the blood of the bull and one goat was brought into the

tabernacle or "tent of meeting," which consisted of three main sections:

- an outer court or courtyard (Exod. 27:9ff.)

- an inner court known as the holy place or "holies" (Exod. 26:33), which featured the altar of incense

- an innermost room known as the most holy place or "holy of holies" (Exod. 26:34), which was separated from the holy place by a veil (Exod. 26:33)[49]

On the Day of Atonement, the two sacrificial phases regarding the bull and one goat took place in the courtyard and the most holy place, respectively. The courtyard featured the altar of sacrifice, the place on which animals were regularly both slaughtered and offered. It was an altar overlaid with bronze and also known as the "altar of burnt offering" (Exod. 40:29). Meanwhile, the most holy place was aptly named, for there God provided his most intimate presence on earth. Flanked by two angels, Yahweh was present upon his mercy seat, which was fixed atop the sacred Ark of the Covenant (Exod. 25:8, 17–22).

So holy was the most holy place that *no* one *entered* it except the high priest, and he only once a year on the Day of Atonement. Any other attempt to enter the most holy place would yield death (Lev. 16:1–2; Num. 3:10; 18:7). In atoning for the sins of Israel and the high priest, the Day of Atonement sacrifices did not begin and end with the slaughter of the bull and one goat on the altar of sacrifice in the courtyard. To *complete* the sacrifices

---

holy of holies. For more on the Day of Atonement sacrifices, see chapter 9.

[49] The tabernacle eventually gave way to the much more ornate Temple, which also had three similar sections.

and thus finish making atonement for Israel's sins, the high priest had to enter the most holy place to offer the sacrificial victims to God, communing with the Almighty by sprinkling their blood in front of and on his mercy seat (Lev. 16:14–15).

Now consider Christ's Sacrifice of Calvary. As with the original Day of Atonement sacrifices, the Sacrifice of Calvary does not begin and end with the slaughter of the victim. That is, the Sacrifice does not begin and end with Jesus' suffering and death on the Cross on Good Friday. That is why we can speak of the Sacrifice *of* Calvary instead of the Sacrifice *on* Calvary: the sacrificial events are not confined to Christ's Passion. When did Jesus enter into the *heavenly* sanctuary with his own body and his own blood? His body remained in his earthly tomb until his Resurrection. And while his Resurrection on Easter Sunday was essential to his Sacrifice (see 1 Cor. 15:17–22),[50] he did not thereby enter into the heavenly sanctuary. After his Resurrection, Jesus told Mary Magdalene that he had "not yet ascended" to his Father (John 20:17). It was only after forty days of appearing to his disciples (see Acts 1:3) that Jesus *completed* the Sacrifice of Calvary by *ascending* into heaven, fulfilling both the Day of Atonement sacrifices in particular and the Old Covenant in general:

> In speaking of a new covenant he treats the first as obsolete. And what is becoming obsolete and growing old is ready to vanish away.... Thus it was necessary for the copies of the heavenly things to be purified with these rites, but the heavenly things themselves with better sacrifices than these. For Christ has entered, not into a

---

[50] See also CCC 645–646, 659.

sanctuary made with hands, a copy of the true one, but into heaven itself, now to appear in the presence of God on our behalf. (Heb. 8:13; 9:23–24)

In summary, without Christ's Ascension and his associated Offering in the heavenly sanctuary, there would be no fulfillment of the Day of Atonement sacrifices and the Old Covenant, and no completion of the Sacrifice begun on Calvary. While there was never any doubt that the divine Christ would complete the mission his Father gave him, we need to make proper sacrificial distinctions. When Christ says, "It is finished" (John 19:30), he refers to the *earthly* phase of his Offering—specifically, the suffering he endured to atone for our sins. Similarly, when the Letter to the Hebrews says Christ does not "offer himself repeatedly," it refers only to Christ's Passion and thus suffering "repeatedly" on the Cross (Heb. 9:25–26; see 1 Pet. 3:18). In other words, Jesus dies only once, and, because he is both victim and priest, he distinctively offers himself to the Father in both phases of his Sacrifice.

But Christ's atonement could not be completed until he ascended to heaven and presented his Self-Offering to the Father, just as the Old Covenant Day of Atonement sacrifices could not have atoned for the sins of Israel had the high priest simply slaughtered the bull and goat, declining to enter the most holy place to present the atoning blood to God.

Given this insight, we can better understand that Christ's Sacrifice did *not* begin and end on Calvary. Scripture affirms the sacrificial importance of Christ's Ascension to the heavenly sanctuary:

But when Christ appeared as a high priest of the good things that have come, ... he entered once for all into the

Holy Place,[51] taking not the blood of goats and calves[52] but his own blood, thus securing an eternal redemption (Heb. 9:1–12). For Christ has entered, not into a sanctuary made with hands, a copy of the true one, but into heaven itself, now to appear in the presence of God on our behalf. Nor was it to offer himself repeatedly, as the high priest enters the Holy Place yearly with blood not his own; for then he would have to suffer repeatedly since the foundation of the world. But as it is, he has appeared once for all at the end of the age to put away sin by the sacrifice of himself. (Heb. 9:24–26)

At his Ascension, Jesus commences the *heavenly* and everlasting phase of his Sacrifice. Our Lord enters not into the earthly Temple, but into the heavenly holy place with the heavenly mercy seat, making intercession on our behalf before his Father and our God. Jesus has achieved an "eternal redemption" so there is no need to suffer again. His was the perfect Sacrifice. And, as the Letter to the Hebrews also conveys, part of sacrificial perfection means having a Sacrifice that keeps on giving, for although Christ has *entered* (past tense) into the heavenly sanctuary at his Ascension, he *continues* "now to appear in the

---

[51] The most holy place, also known as "the holy of holies," is sometimes referred to as "the holy place," but with the clear stipulation that this is the holy place *within the veil*, as opposed to the holy place *outside the veil* (compare Exodus 26:33–35 with Leviticus 16:11–19 and Heb. 9:11–25). Of course, in the heavenly sanctuary (Heb. 9:12), there can be no veiled barriers between God and man, only a most holy place where man dwells face-to-face with God (see Cor. 12:8–12).

[52] "Calves" is a collective reference to the young bulls offered year after year on the Day of Atonement.

presence of God on our behalf" (Heb. 9:24). One should expect an infinitely powerful and therefore perpetual Sacrifice when the priest and victim is the omnipotent, eternal Son of God.[53]

Indeed, because it culminates in glory in the timeless heavenly sanctuary, Christ's Sacrifice is necessarily a perpetual, ongoing Sacrifice. The *earthly, historical phase* (suffering, death, Resurrection) has certainly come and gone. We are not to expect a repeat performance of these actions a second, third, or fourth time, and so on, nor does the Church teach that Christ suffers, dies, and rises anew at every Mass. However, the *heavenly phase*, which began with Christ's Self-Offering in the heavenly sanctuary and which completed the Sacrifice of Calvary, never ends. That is why we can speak of Christ, currently in heaven, reigning in glory as "a Lamb standing, as though it had been slain" (Rev. 5:6). The heavenly phase mysteriously brings Christ's death and Resurrection into a sanctuary "not made with hands" at the Ascension (Heb. 9:11–12; see 9:23–24). As a result, in offering himself to the Father in the heavenly sanctuary, Jesus bears the marks of his Crucifixion while simultaneously reigning in glory. He exhibits the wounds of his having once been slain, yet he *stands*, illustrating that he has triumphed over sin and death![54]

---

[53] "The Day of Atonement is the only possible source of the 'both high priest and victim' belief associated with the Eucharist," writes Dr. Margaret Barker, a British Protestant Bible scholar, in her article "The Temple Roots of the Liturgy." For example, "Origen interpreted the Eucharist as the Day of Atonement offering: 'Christ the true high priest who made atonement for you ... hear him saying to you: "This is my blood which is poured out for you for the forgiveness of sins"'" (*On Leviticus* 9)."

[54] "In the heavenly sanctuary," Fr. Nicholas Gihr writes, "Christ appears there as high priest and mediator before the face of God, and, interceding for us. He presents to Him His wounds and His

Scripture affirms that "every high priest is appointed to offer gifts and sacrifices; hence it is necessary for this priest [Jesus] also to have something to offer" (Heb. 8:3). Notice that the Letter to the Hebrews uses the present tense — "offer" — and that it is speaking of Christ's heavenly activity *after* his death on the Cross, for it describes Jesus as "a high priest, one who is seated at the right hand of the throne of the Majesty in heaven, a minister in the [heavenly] sanctuary and the true tent which is set up not by man but by the Lord" (Heb. 8:1–2). In addition, the Letter to the Hebrews further affirms that Jesus' priesthood *continues* in heaven, for he "holds his priesthood permanently" and thus "always lives to make intercession" for us (Heb. 7:24–25). And even though Scripture does say Jesus "sat down at the right hand" of the Father (Mark 16:19), this expression regarding his triumphant entry into heaven as the King of kings certainly does not imply that his priestly ministry has concluded, as Hebrews 8:1–2 makes clear; again, although he "*has entered*" the heavenly sanctuary, he continues "*now* to appear in the presence of God on our behalf" (Heb. 9:24, emphasis added; see Heb. 10:12; see CCC 1090 and 1326).

What does Christ the permanent priest offer his Father in "always living to make intercession" for us? The Bible makes mention of only one priestly Sacrifice that Jesus made — his definitive, "once for all" Self-Offering (Heb. 7:27; 9:28). Because the Bible also says Jesus continues to offer something to the Father in heaven, we must conclude that the Sacrifice of Calvary

---

bloody death in order to apply to us the fruits of redemption" (Rev. Dr. Nicholas Gihr, *The Holy Sacrifice of the Mass: Dogmatically, Liturgically, and Ascetically Explained*, translated from the German (St. Louis: B. Herder, 1949), 700.

culminated in everlasting glory at the Ascension. That is, he continues to offer what he first offered at his Ascension—his perfected Self-Offering.[55]

That Was Then, This Is Now (and Forever!)

The Sacrifice of Calvary fulfills all Old Covenant sacrifices (CCC 1330), particularly the two most important: Passover and the Day of Atonement. But how does Jesus make this perpetual, heavenly Sacrifice present on earth at Mass? Because of the heavenly, never-ending nature of Christ's one Sacrifice, the biblical concept of "remembrance" becomes much more extraordinary in celebrating the *New Covenant* Passover, the Mass, which Jesus first celebrated at the Last Supper (see Luke 22:15). In the Old Covenant Passover, the Israelites would relive the original Passover, but it would be an imperfect remembrance. They would experience God's enduring covenant blessing in the present and thus become present, in one sense, to the original event that initiated the Exodus; however, *each year* the Israelites would always have to sacrifice *new* Passover lambs. As noted earlier, in terms of the contributions of its human and animal participants, the original Passover would always remain a limited, past event. Moses could not always return to oversee the liturgical celebration, and the original lambs could not be brought back for additional sacrificial duty.

---

[55] As a divine Person, Jesus is perfect, but he took on our human nature to perfect it and to redeem us (Heb. 2:10; see 5:8–10; 10:10; CCC 412). See Fr. James Swetnam, S.J., "Christology and the Eucharist in the Epistle to the Hebrews," *Biblica* 70, no. 1 (1989): 74–95.

In contrast, in the New Covenant, there is only one Lamb, who died "once for all" (Heb. 7:27; 9:28), and yet whose one Sacrifice also has a perpetual, "once for all" character. In other words, because the principal human participant who consummated the New Covenant is also God, his original Self-Offering can become present to us again and again. Indeed, because there is only one Lamb, whose Sacrifice culminates in everlasting glory, both the original divine blessing *and* the original Passover Sacrifice endure in the New Covenant, making Christ's once-for-all Self-Offering present *every time* we celebrate the Mass "in memory" of him. More profound yet, because Christ's Sacrifice is principally offered in the heavenly sanctuary, we can also say that heaven and earth mysteriously intersect at Mass, enabling us to become present to his everlasting Offering. In other words, a foretaste of heaven is as close as the next Mass at your local church!

Realizing that the Sacrifice of Calvary, similar to the Day of Atonement, has distinct, yet inseparable phases[56]— including a heavenly, everlasting one — helps us better understand how the Mass can be reoffered or re-presented time and again. Unlike the Old Covenant Day of Atonement, in which the priest would enter and depart from the sanctuary every year, Jesus entered the *heavenly* sanctuary at the Ascension once for all, *yet remains* to continue ministering as a priest. Indeed, Christ *remains* in heaven, holding "his priesthood permanently," and "he always

---

[56] As noted, the Resurrection can be considered part of the earthly phase of Christ's Sacrifice, but also a unique, distinct aspect, since only with his Sacrifice is there a Resurrection between the two traditional sacrificial aspects of first slaughtering the victim and then completing the offering of it to God.

lives to make intercession" for us (Heb. 7:24–25) until his Second Coming.[57] He remains in heaven, and yet the power of his priesthood is felt on earth, for he makes intercession for us as a priest forever according to the order of Melchizedek (see Heb. 5:10; 7:17), making his Sacrifice sacramentally present at every Mass under the Melchizedekian appearances of bread and wine. Thus, in the Mass, as the *Catechism* conveys, Christ's everlasting priestly ministry unites and fulfills both the Passover and the redemptive Day of Atonement sacrifices:

> In the New Testament, the [Passover] memorial takes on new meaning. When the Church celebrates the Eucharist, she commemorates Christ's Passover, and it is made present: the sacrifice Christ offered once for all on the cross remains ever present [cf. Heb. 7:25–27]. "As often as the sacrifice of the Cross by which 'Christ our Pasch has been sacrificed' is celebrated on the altar, the work of our redemption is carried out." (CCC 1364, quoting *LG* 3; cf. 1 Cor. 5:7)

The Sacrifice of Calvary: Not Limited by Time

The Mass is a miraculous event in which heaven and earth intersect, for Catholic priests act in the person and power of Christ. The Mass is not Calvary repeated, as if Christ were crucified again, but is rather the re-presentation, or making present

---

[57] Jesus' intercession for our salvation will culminate at his Second Coming when he returns to earth in glory for the Last Judgment (see CCC 1038–1041). Yet he will continue to intercede for us with the Father, for he is the new and everlasting mediator of the New and everlasting Covenant. Indeed, Jesus' Self-Offering to the Father on our behalf is everlasting.

on earth, of "Calvary completed," a Sacrifice that began with Christ's suffering and death on Calvary but culminated in everlasting glory when he presented his Self-Sacrifice to his Father in the timeless realm of the heavenly sanctuary. That is, the Mass makes present the completed, glorified Sacrifice of Christ that he forever offers to the Father in heaven. While his glorified Body and Blood are offered at Mass under the sacramental appearances of bread and wine, the earthly sacrificial phase of shedding his blood is not repeated, and thus at each Mass, as the Council of Trent teaches, "the same Christ who offered himself once in a bloody manner on the altar of the cross is contained and offered in an unbloody manner."[58]

We grasp the depth of this mystery when we further ponder the wonder of the Last Supper itself. The Last Supper is an offering of Christ's Body and Blood that historically *preceded* his Self-Offering of Calvary. The God who created time is not limited by time. The same God who can culminate his Self-Offering in everlasting glory in the heavenly sanctuary at his Ascension can also, being all powerful, offer this same completed, glorified Sacrifice[59] in *advance* of his actual historical death and Resurrection. For, at the Last Supper, what Jesus lived out once in history was *prepresented* and *anticipated* in sacramental mystery. Similarly, we who live *after* the historical Passion and glory of

---

[58] Council of Trent (1562: *Doctrina de Ss. Missae Sacrificio*: "Doctrine Concerning the Sacrifice of the Mass"), chap. 2: DS 1743, quoted in CCC 1367.

[59] See also Msgr. Anthony A. La Femina, S.T.L., J.C.D., *Eucharist and Covenant in John's Last Supper (Jn. 12:44–17:26)* (New Hope, KY: New Hope Publications, 2000), 43–67. Also see the appendix.

Christ's death and Resurrection are actually able to *re-present* in mystery this *very same Sacrifice*.[60]

Here Comes the Son

In celebrating Mass, we can also say that *we* become present to the timeless Sacrifice of Calvary, because you cannot repeat that which transcends time and thus never ends. Consider this analogy as a means of further clarification. The sun does not rise anew each day like the legendary Phoenix bird, which repeatedly rises from its ashes to new life on a daily basis. Rather, the sun exists *perpetually within* time, and *we* become present anew to our earth-sustaining life source each day at sunrise, as our world turns on its axis. Similarly, Jesus, the Son of God, does not suffer, die, and rise again at each and every Mass, as some Protestant Christians misunderstand. Rather, the completed Sacrifice of the Lamb who was slain *transcends time itself* and thus is celebrated *forever* in heaven (see Rev. 5:11–14). Therefore, every time we "remember" Jesus at Mass, we are able to become present to — and re-present anew to the Father — the never-ending and eternally life-giving Offering of his Son. While time passes, Christ's Sacrifice of Calvary remains the same (see Heb. 13:8), the quintessential gift that keeps on giving:

> In the liturgy of the Church, it is principally his own Paschal mystery that Christ signifies and makes present. During his earthly life Jesus announced his Paschal mystery by his teaching and anticipated it by his actions. When his Hour comes, he lives out the unique event

[60] Similarly, Christ applied the merits of his Sacrifice to his Blessed Mother in advance of Calvary, preserving her from sin from the moment of her conception.

of history that does not pass away: Jesus dies, is buried, rises from the dead, and is seated at the right hand of the Father "once for all" [Rom. 6:10; Heb. 7:27; 9:12; cf. John 13:1; 17:1]. His Paschal mystery is a real event that occurred in our history, but it is unique: all other historical events happen once, and then they pass away, swallowed up in the past. The Paschal mystery of Christ, by contrast, cannot remain only in the past, because by his death he destroyed death, and all that Christ is—all that he did and suffered for all men—participates in the divine eternity, and so transcends all times while being made present in them all. The event of the Cross and Resurrection *abides* and draws everything toward life. (CCC 1085, emphasis in original)

In summary, Christ's Sacrifice that began on Calvary cannot be isolated from its liturgical completion in heaven. As Frank Sheed concisely observed, "The essence of the Mass is that Christ is making an offering to the Father of Himself, who was slain for us upon Calvary. The Mass is Calvary, *as Christ now offers it to His Father*."[61]

Questions for Reflection and Discussion

1. (a) What is the difference between how Americans recall the Fourth of July and how ancient Israelites "remembered" Passover each year? (b) Explain the crucial role of God's action in Israel's remembering.

---

[61] Frank Sheed, *Theology and Sanity*, 2nd ed. (San Francisco: Ignatius Press, 1993), 332, emphasis in original.

2. (a) How can the Church re-present Jesus' Sacrifice again and again, even though our Lord died "once for all"? Besides discussion of Scripture passages, see also CCC 1085. (b) What scriptural evidence exists that Christ's priesthood continues *now* in heaven? (c) Because the principal ministry of priests is to offer sacrifices (Heb. 5:1; 8:3), and because the Bible notes that Jesus offered only one Sacrifice—that is, once for all—could Jesus now be offering in heaven a sacrifice other than Calvary completed? (d) If the answer to (c) is yes, would that necessarily imply an insufficiency of the Sacrifice of Calvary and thereby demean Christ and his work? Explain. (e) If the answer to (c) is yes, would that also make Christ's heavenly ministry anticlimactic or inferior to what he achieved on earth? Explain. (f) Can an answer of yes to (c) really be reconciled with the scriptural data? Explain.

2. (a) In light of your answers to questions 1 and 2, how is "remembering" crucially different in the New Covenant Passover from the Old Covenant Passover? (b) Christ could not have "remembered" his Sacrifice of Calvary at the Last Supper since Calvary had not yet taken place. So, what was he doing at the Last Supper? Could Jesus really pre-present and anticipate his Sacrifice? Why or why not? Asked another way, could an omnipotent God create something—namely, time—that could thereafter limit his salvific, priestly actions on earth?

3. The Mass has been described as our becoming present to the everlasting Sacrifice of Christ. (a) How does the analogy of the sun illustrate this view? (b) How is the analogy of the Phoenix bird, which some Christians erroneously view as an apt comparison for what Catholics believe about the Mass, actually a caricature of the Mass?

8

"They Shall Eat the Flesh"
The Passover as Communion Sacrifice

Background Reading
  Genesis 26:23–33; 31:44–54
  Exodus 12; 24:1–12
  Luke 22
  Hebrews 7–9
  Jeremiah 31:31–34
  Ezekiel 36:24–36
  Colossians 2:11–14
  Exodus 16
  John 6
  1 Corinthians 11

In laying the liturgical groundwork for what we today call the Mass, God instituted the Passover as a *communion* sacrifice —that is, one in which Israel ate lambs in communion with God after offering them. In Genesis, we see communion meals eaten in connection with Isaac's covenant with the Philistine King Abimelech (Gen. 26:23–33) and Jacob's covenant with his father-in-law, Laban (Gen. 31:44–54; see Exod. 24:9–11). Communion meals—that is, ones that typically involved face-to-face meetings with conversation and food—strengthened family bonds and sometimes even reconciled enemies. With the Passover, the communion with God was very real, even though the Almighty did not draw near for face-to-face conversation with the Israelite community.

As noted in the last chapter, God commanded the Israelites to eat no ordinary lamb. A Passover lamb, either a goat or sheep of one year (Exod. 12:5), was to be without blemish, that is, possess no visible physical defects. Any blemish at all would disqualify a lamb from fulfilling the prescriptions of the Passover. As if to respect its pristine state, God also directed that a Passover lamb be carefully prepared and eaten, without breaking any of its bones (Exod. 12:46).

The Israelites served the roasted lambs with bitter herbs and unleavened bread (Exod. 12:8–11), reminding them of their hardships in and emancipation from Egypt, and how God continued the blessing of that first Passover in their own lives. Passover also marked the beginning of the feast of Unleavened Bread, also known as Mazzoth or Azymes (Exod. 12:15–19; see Matt. 26:17; Mark 14:12). Beginning on Passover evening, the Israelites would eat only unleavened bread for seven consecutive days. This feast reinforced the memory of the Passover, reminding the Israelites of their ancestors' hasty departure out of northern Egypt that began the Exodus. Because Moses and his fellow Israelites had to leave Egypt in such a hurry after the divine destruction of that country's firstborn, there was not enough time to let the bread rise, and thus no leaven was added (see Exod. 12:8, 11–13).

A Memorable Menu

The Passover meal renewed and strengthened Israel's covenant bond with God, but there was an additional, unique element:

God designed the menu so that future generations could better remember and reexperience the original events that set their ancestors free:

> [W]hen your children say to you, "What do you mean by this service?" you shall say, "It is the Lord's passover, for he passed over the houses of the people of Israel in Egypt, when he slew the Egyptians but spared our houses.... [F]or with a strong hand the Lord has brought you out of Egypt." (Exod. 12:26–27; 13:9)

And so the tradition began in which the youngest son participating in a Passover would ask the male head of his family, such as his father or grandfather, to explain and interpret the significance of the meal (Exod. 13:8–10). While the Passover rite is not elaborated on extensively in Scripture, other Jewish writings illustrate that the Passover meal was used to explain the original celebration of the rite and its historical context. In the Jewish Mishnah,[62] we read, "Whosoever does not mention (in his interpretation) the following three things at the Passover meal has failed in his duty: the paschal lamb, the unleavened bread, and the bitter herbs; cf. Exodus 12:8" (Pesahim 10, 5).[63] Later in that same passage, the Mishnah provides an explanation of each element of the meal:

> The paschal lamb (should be interpreted as follows): because God passed over (*pasah*) in mercy the houses of our

---

[62] The Mishnah is the part of the Talmud that contains oral laws based on the Pentateuch. For more information, please see page 76, n. 46.

[63] As cited in Joachim Jeremias, *The Eucharistic Words of Jesus*, trans. Rev. Arnold Ehrhardt (Oxford, UK: Basil Blackwell, 1955), 32.

fathers in Egypt, Exodus 12:27; the bitter herbs: because the Egyptians made bitter the life of our fathers in Egypt, Exodus 1:14; the unleavened bread: because our fathers were delivered out of Egypt (in such haste, that there was no time left to wait for the leavening of the dough), Exodus 12:39 (Pesahim 10, 5).[64]

Changing the Menu:
A New Lamb Makes a Permanent Appearance

At the Last Supper, Jesus reordered the significance of Passover not around an event of the distant past, but mysteriously around *one that had not yet taken place in history*—his imminent suffering and death on Calvary on Good Friday. Thus, Matthew, Mark, and Luke provide a transformed explanation of the lamb, bitter herbs, and unleavened bread of the Passover meal. The traditional lamb is conspicuously absent from their Last Supper accounts, and the bread and wine[65] that had traditionally been part of the Passover gain great importance with Jesus' Offering. Because the focus is on the Passover Lamb of God, who sacrifices himself for the sin of the world (see John 1:29–36; 1 Cor. 5:7–8), the bread and the wine are invested with new and greater significance. At the Last Supper, Jesus demonstrates that, as God, he is not limited by the time he has created; he miraculously institutes the Mass, both anticipating the free offering of

---

[64] Jeremias, *The Eucharistic Words of Jesus*, 32.

[65] While not explicitly mentioned in the Passover prescriptions of Exodus 12, wine was the typical drink with ritual meals in ancient Israel, and, as Jewish tradition testifies, four cups of wine became an integral part of the Passover meal, also known as the Seder meal.

his life and prepresenting the glorified, completed Sacrifice of Calvary under the sacramental forms of bread and wine (see CCC 610–611):

> And he took bread, and when he had given thanks he broke it and gave it to them, saying, "This is my body which is given for you. Do this in remembrance of me." And likewise the cup after supper, saying, "This cup which is poured out for you is the new covenant in my blood." (Luke 22:19–20)

At the Last Supper, Jesus celebrated Passover with the traditional matter of unleavened bread and cups of wine, but, when he associated these elements with himself, their substance was miraculously transubstantiated into his Body and his Blood while maintaining the sacramental forms (that is, appearances) of mere bread and wine (see CCC 1364, 1376–1377). The Passover concept of remembering—*anamnesis* in Greek—took on a profound, new meaning with Jesus. Before the Last Supper, the lamb, bread, and wine would recall the first such items offered or consumed, or both, at the inaugural Passover while invoking God's enduring blessing in the present. At the Last Supper, the bread and wine *became* the Lamb of God, as Jesus prepresented and anticipated his Sacrifice. Similarly, after Calvary the Mass is not simply an "action which causes remembrance,"[66] but one that makes present the *same, identical* Passover Sacrifice of Calvary, although, as at the Last Supper, in its completed, glorified state under the form of a sacrament.[67]

---

[66] Léon-Dufour, *Sharing the Eucharistic Bread*, 109–110; see 109–116.
[67] For further reading on the Eucharist offered at the Last Supper as a completed Sacrifice, see the appendix.

Jesus fulfilled the Passover ordinance as the definitive Lamb of God, delivering God's people not from a mere human oppressor — Egypt — but from sin, death and the devil (see CCC 421, 635–636, 1337–1340). There would be no need to shed any more blood. Yet, because the Passover remains "an ordinance for ever," we remember at each Mass the bitter Passion Christ suffered on Calvary to deliver us from sin and death, much as the Old Covenant Passover remembered the sacrifice that delivered Israel from the bitter bondage of Egyptian slavery. However, whereas the Old Covenant Passover did not make present the sacrificial lambs first offered in Egypt, the New Covenant Passover always makes present — under the sacramental species of bread and wine — the selfsame Sacrifice of Calvary by which the Lamb of God delivered us from sin and death. And then, true to the Passover ordinance tradition, we are blessed to partake of that same divine Lamb.[68]

Christ has no need "to suffer repeatedly" (Heb. 9:26), for he died "once for all" (Heb. 7:26–28). But, as noted in the last chapter, he also completed his Sacrifice by entering the heavenly

---

[68] As Pope John Paul notes in his 2003 encyclical *Ecclesia de Eucharistia*, no. 52, "Saint John Chrysostom put it well: 'We always offer the same Lamb, not one today and another tomorrow, but always the same one. For this reason the sacrifice is always only one.... Even now we offer that victim who was once offered and who will never be consumed.'" (The pope cites Chrysostom's *Homilies on the Epistle to Hebrews*, Homily 17, 3.) In saying the victim will "never be consumed," Chrysostom is noting that Christ's Sacrifice is perpetual and therefore inexhaustible; it cannot be "consumed" in the sense that it will never expire. As a faithful Catholic bishop, though, the saint is certainly not denying that the faithful consume (that is, eat and drink) the Eucharistic Communion Sacrifice of Christ's Body and Blood.

sanctuary "once for all" at his Ascension (Heb. 9:12), meaning his Sacrifice of Calvary culminated in everlasting glory and therefore continues for all eternity. This is what Scripture means when it says that Jesus "always lives to make intercession for" us (Heb. 7:23–25). As a heavenly high priest, Jesus must have something to offer (Heb. 8:3, 6), and the only sacrifice it can be is his perpetual and most powerful Self-Offering, a Sacrifice that we are most blessed to re-present and partake of at Mass, the New Covenant Passover.

Come One, Come All

Straying from the Old Covenant Passover meal plan had serious consequences. If anyone ate leavened bread during the seven-day period, he would be cut off from the congregation of Israel (Exod. 12:15, 19). This brings us to the Passover guest list. At first glance, God's directive might sound like an exclusive, modern-day country club: "No foreigner shall eat of it.... No sojourner or hired servant may eat of it" (Exod. 12:43, 45). Unlike today's "members only" clubs, though, God did not erect barriers that only the very rich and powerful could surmount. If you wanted to partake of the Passover, the choice was ultimately *yours*. Whether you were a slave or a stranger or sojourner—that is, a foreigner fraternizing with Israel—you simply had to say yes to God and all of his laws (Exod. 12:44, 48). Making that choice—and sticking with it—was not easy, but it was a prudent choice. God had proven himself by liberating his people from the mighty Egyptians, drawing many newcomers who wanted to share in that freedom and fellowship with his people.

To gain access to Passover fellowship, both Israelite and non-Israelite men had to pay the additional "admission price" of circumcision. Circumcision was the sacramental expression by which non-Israelites could pledge their covenant allegiance to Yahweh. Having fulfilled that painful prerequisite, the slave or sojourner was treated as a "native of the land" and a member of the "congregation of Israel" (Exod. 12:47–48). As Moses proclaimed, "There shall be *one* law for the native and for the stranger who sojourns among you" (Exod. 12:50, emphasis added).

Obedience to God's law, including a type of circumcision, remained a prerequisite for the New Covenant Passover, but the pain of circumcision stemmed from repentance of sin, not a flint knife (see Josh. 5:2). Everyone in Israel would receive this new circumcision, which God would administer to their hearts, not their bodies, as he first foretold to Moses (see Deut. 30:6). Jeremiah prophesied about this "new covenant" in which God would write his law upon the hearts of the Israelites and forgive all their sins (Jer. 31:31–34). Ezekiel also prophesied that God would cleanse the Israelites from all their iniquities, providing them with both a new heart and a new spirit (Ezek. 36:24–36). The prophet added that this cleansing and reception of God's Spirit would come via sprinkling (Ezek. 36:25), a ritual that Jesus would call baptism. St. Paul elaborates in his Letter to the Colossians:

> In him also you were circumcised with a circumcision made without hands, by putting off the body of flesh in the circumcision of Christ; and you were buried with him in baptism, in which you were also raised with him through faith in the working of God, who raised him from the dead. And you, who were dead in trespasses and the uncircumcision of the flesh, God made alive together with him, having forgiven us all our trespasses, having canceled the bond which stood against us with its legal demands; this he set aside, nailing it to the cross. (Col. 2:11–14)

When Christ proved himself on the Cross, the New Covenant Passover—like the Old—also became attractive, drawing disciples from all nations (see Matt. 28:18–20).

Living Forever on the Lamb of God

In the New Covenant Passover meal, Christ fulfills the typology of the Passover lamb. While battered and bruised for our sins (see Isa. 53:5; 1 Pet. 2:24–25), Jesus is unblemished in a much more important sense: he is without stain of sin (Heb. 4:15). In addition, when Jesus offered himself on Calvary, God made sure the Roman soldiers observed another Passover prescription, for they broke none of his bones (John 19:36).

Jesus fulfills other Old Testament motifs. As the bread-like manna sustained ancient Israel en route to its earthly Promised Land (see Exod. 16:31–32), so too Christ, "the true bread from heaven" (John 6:32), leads us to our eternal paradise: "I am the living bread which came down from heaven; if anyone eats of this bread, he will live for ever; and the bread which I shall give for the life of the world is my flesh" (John 6:51). Thus, Jesus became not only the perfect Passover Sacrifice for our sins, but also the perfect Passover meal to sustain us spiritually unto heaven (see John 6:54–58).

All are welcome to share full communion in the New Passover, but they must freely embrace membership in Christ's Church (see CCC 815). Catholics themselves cannot presume upon their relationship with God, for, like their Old Covenant predecessors, they remain free to maintain or break communion with God. Violating Old Covenant Passover meal norms would cut you off in ancient Israel, but profaning God's Body and Blood by receiving the Eucharist in a state of mortal sin could cost you both your earthly life and your immortal soul:

Whoever, therefore, eats the bread or drinks the cup of the
Lord in an unworthy manner will be guilty of profaning
the body and blood of the Lord. Let a man examine himself, and so eat of the bread and drink of the cup. For any
one who eats and drinks without discerning the body eats
and drinks judgment upon himself. That is why many of
you are weak and ill, and some have died. But if we judged
ourselves truly, we should not be judged. But when we are
judged by the Lord, we are chastened so that we may not
be condemned along with the world. (1 Cor 11:27–32)

New Covenant Passover:
Communion Sacrifice or Simply Memorial Supper?

Christians would have no anxiety about being "condemned
along with the world" if their salvation were irrevocably assured
by simply accepting Jesus as Lord and Savior at a given moment.
And if the Lord's Supper involved simply eating and drinking
mere bread and wine, it is hard to imagine how these staples of
ancient life could lead to infirmity and death, for even natural
food sustains life. Physical death would be conceivable only with
a fatal additive. Even then, "profaning the body and blood" of
Christ makes no sense if one is consuming only bread, wine, and
some death-dealing additive.

In considering St. Paul's words and other biblical data about
the Passover, we see a profound difference between the two com-
peting claimants to the title of fulfilled New Covenant Passover:
the Catholic Mass and the Protestant Lord's Supper. Almost all
Protestants believe that Christ's Sacrifice cannot be re-presented
at Mass, although some believe that we partake of Christ in
some fashion in the Eucharist. Protestants generally believe
that, whereas Christ's Sacrifice of Calvary was essential to their

salvation, Christians appropriate the gift of salvation through accepting Christ as Lord and Savior, not at all by partaking of the sacrament of Baptism or the Lord's Supper. If we accept these premises, the conclusion follows logically: even if we could do so, there is no point in re-presenting Christ's Sacrifice, let alone partaking of that Sacrifice, because our salvation is assured by accepting Christ as our Savior on a single occasion, or, as other Protestants would argue, by simply continuing in right relationship with Christ after the initial acceptance of his gift of salvation.

If the New Covenant Passover has truly nothing to do with our salvation, though, then the Old Covenant Passover becomes, oddly enough, relatively more dramatic and life-giving than its New Covenant successor. The New Covenant Passover ordinance becomes an anticlimactic ritual that we keep out of obedience, not because of its salvific benefit for ourselves and others (see CCC 1391–1401).

The words of St. Paul to the Corinthians, our Lord's recorded words in John 6, and other biblical evidence convey a much different story. The New Covenant Passover—that is, the Mass or Divine Liturgy—provides eternal life through a deeply intimate encounter with Christ; thus, partaking of it in an unworthy manner can compound one's state of mortal sin and thereby possibly yield eternal loss (see CCC 1385, 1861). The Mass is no mere memory or meal. Rather, as Archbishop Fulton J. Sheen said, the Mass re-presents the greatest event in the history of the world in which we, as members of Christ's one Mystical Body, the Church, are most blessed to take part. His words are worth quoting at length to conclude this chapter:

> The most sublime act in the history of Christ was His *Death*. Death is always important for it seals a destiny....

Everyone else who was ever born into the world, came into it to *live*; our Lord came into it to *die*. Death was a stumbling block to the life of Socrates, but it was the crown to the life of Christ. He Himself told us that He came "to give His Life as a redemption for many"; that no one could take away His Life; but He would lay it down of Himself.

If then Death was the supreme moment for which Christ lived, it was therefore the *one thing* He wished to have remembered. He did not ask that men should write down His Words into a Scripture; He did not ask that His kindness to the poor should be recorded in history; but He did ask that men remember His Death. And in order that its memory not be any haphazard narrative on the part of men, He Himself instituted the precise way it should be recalled.

The Church which Christ founded has not only preserved the Word He spoke, and the wonders He wrought; it has also taken Him seriously when He said: "Do this for a commemoration of me." And that action whereby we re-enact His Death on the Cross *is* the Sacrifice of the Mass, in which we do as a memorial what He did at the Last Supper as the prefiguration of His Passion.

Hence the Mass is to us the crowning act of Christian worship.... The *altar*, and not the pulpit or the choir or the organ, is the center of worship, for there *is* re-enacted [that is, re-presented] the memorial of His Passion. Its value does not depend on him who *says* it, or on him who hears it; it depends on Him who is the One High Priest and Victim, Jesus Christ our Lord....

The Sacrifice of the Cross is not something which happened nineteen hundred years ago [today almost two thousand years ago]. It is still happening. It is not something past like the signing of the Declaration of Independence; it is an abiding drama on which the curtain has not yet rung down. Let it not be believed that it happened a long time ago, and therefore no more concerns us than anything else in the past. *Calvary belongs to all times and to all places.*[69]

Questions for Reflection and Discussion

1. St. Paul describes Jesus as "Christ, our paschal lamb" (1 Cor. 5:7), that is, our Passover lamb. In the Old Covenant, the Passover was both a sacrifice and a meal. (a) What type of sacrifice, therefore, is the Passover sacrifice? (b) Considering Jesus' actions at the Last Supper, is the New Covenant Passover he celebrated also a communion sacrifice? Explain.

2. (a) What were the three major elements of a Passover meal in the Old Covenant? (b) How did these elements help the Israelites remember and reexperience the annual feast?

3. (a) How did Jesus modify the Passover menu, particularly regarding the lamb served? (b) How did he invest new meaning in the bread and wine served at the meal?

4. (a) What were/are the prerequisites to partake of the Passover sacrifice in both the Old and New Covenants, respectively? (b) Why is being in full communion with the Church, and not

---

[69] Archbishop Fulton J. Sheen, *Calvary and the Mass* (New York: P. J. Kenedy and Sons, 1936; retypeset and republished by Coalition in Support of *Ecclesia Dei*, 1996), 9–12, emphasis in original.

simply being a Christian, crucial for one to have regular access to the New Covenant Passover? (Hint: read CCC 1398–1400.)

5. (a) How are we able to partake of the *same* Sacrifice at every Mass? (b) In 1 Corinthians 11:27–34, Paul says that some have suffered and died because of unworthy reception of the Eucharist. Yet, what is the worst possible consequence of such unworthy reception? (See CCC 1385, 1861.)

6. (a) What is the general Protestant view of the significance of the New Covenant Passover? (b) Can such a view be reconciled with St. Paul's words in 1 Corinthians 11? (c) What other biblical evidence supports the Catholic view that consuming the Eucharist is a real partaking of the Body, Blood, Soul, and Divinity of Christ in his one sacrifice, with implications for salvation? (d) How does Archbishop Fulton Sheen make the case for the Catholic view of the New Covenant Passover?

9

God Draws Near to His People

Ancient Israel as Liturgical Training Ground

Background Reading
  Exodus 19:4–6
  Exodus 24:1–11
  Leviticus 8:22–30
  1 Corinthians 10:1–22; 11:23–34
  Matthew 26:1–35
  Luke 22:1–23
  Exodus 25–26
  Exodus 29:38–46
  Leviticus 16
  Exodus 12:1–14
  Isaiah 52:7–12, 53:1–12
  John 3:12–15
  Hebrews 5:5–10; 7:23–28; 8:1–3; 9:11–14; 23–28; 10:1–14

While the biblical story of the Mass fittingly begins in the book of Genesis, Exodus and Leviticus thereafter advance its most important Old Testament themes. Other books have their part, but the major story lines are rooted in these two books, with their coverage of the Exodus from Egypt and Yahweh's subsequent provision of the Old Covenant Law. The Book of Exodus is particularly dense with Eucharistic types and motifs. We have already considered the importance of the Passover, and, in chapter 10, we will briefly examine the manna that prefigures Jesus as the Eucharistic Bread come down from heaven. In this chapter, we will consider:

Book of Exodus

- the sealing of the Old Covenant on Mount Sinai, which prefigures Jesus' inauguration of the New Covenant at the Last Supper and through living out his Sacrifice

- the wilderness tabernacle, which preceded the Temple in housing God's ongoing, intimate presence among Israel and, one might argue, prefigures the church buildings in which our Lord maintains his unique Eucharistic Presence in the tabernacle

- the twice-daily offering of lambs at the tabernacle known as the Tamid ("perpetual") sacrifice, which prefigures the daily offering of the Eucharistic Lamb of God at Mass

Book of Leviticus

- Yom Kippur (the Day of Atonement), the one day each year when the high priest would enter the tabernacle's most holy place and intercede intimately with God, offering sacrifices for his own and Israel's sins. This solemn feast prefigures Christ's definitive Offering of Calvary for all mankind.

Hear, O Israel!

In leading the Hebrews out of Egypt to the Promised Land, Yahweh had more in mind than upgrading Israel's real-estate holdings. A nation needs its own land, but Israel, like any other nation, was more in need of its God than possessing its own geographical boundaries. Central to Israel's national identity was its relationship with God, for Yahweh had long ago sworn to Abraham that *he* would make a great nation of the patriarch's descendants (Gen. 12:2). Now, with Israel having emerged from its four-hundred-year bondage in Egypt (see Gen. 15:13–15), God made a covenant with the Hebrews, providing a series of laws in Exodus 20–23, the most important of which were the enduring Ten Commandments (20:1–17). After coming down from Mount Sinai, Moses announced God's laws and the people pledged to follow them (Exod. 24:1–3). Moses proceeded to write down all of God's words, rising the next day and sealing the covenant in an elaborate ceremony (Exod. 24:4–11).

Several hallmarks distinguish the Old Covenant's ratification and anticipate the consummation of the New Covenant. For example, God ratified both covenants at mountains: the Old at Sinai, in the southern Sinai Peninsula; the New on Mount Zion, that is, Jerusalem. We will examine other covenant parallels in more detail:

- Both involve a chief mediator between man and God: Moses in the Old Covenant and Jesus in the New.

- Both involve representatives of the twelve tribes of Israel: the nation gathered at the foot of Sinai for the Old and the twelve apostles in the Upper Room for the New.

- The "blood of the covenant" seals both.

- Jesus ordains the apostles as priests during the Last Supper, and it appears that Moses may have performed an ordination ceremony in Exodus 24.

• Both include a communion meal between God and his people.

Moses stood out in Israel as a confidant of God, for only he could draw near to the Lord for intimate conversation (Exod. 24:2). The Lord called Moses to mediate his covenant with his people and teach them his ways. After the Exodus, Moses received God's law atop Mount Sinai and served as Israel's chief governing authority, as those who opposed him were harshly reminded. When Aaron and Miriam protested their brother Moses' authority and his marriage to a darker-skinned, Cushite woman, Miriam became white with leprosy (Num. 12:1–16). When Korah and his fellow Levitical rebels tried to topple Moses' rule over Israel, God inflicted capital punishment on them (Num. 16:1–35).

Moses also served as priestly mediator in ratifying God's covenant with Israel. After he received God's law, the people gathered together at the foot of Mount Sinai to become God's nation. God had sworn to Abraham that he would make a great nation of his descendants, and now he was about to make it official in a solemn ceremony. Moses built an altar at the foot of the mountain and erected twelve pillars to represent the twelve tribes of Israel. He then directed the young men of Israel to offer burnt offerings and peace offerings to God. Half of the sacrificial blood Moses put in basins, and the other half he threw against the altar:

> Then he took the book of the covenant, and read it in the hearing of the people; and they said, "All that the Lord has spoken we will do, and we will be obedient." And Moses took the blood and threw it upon the people, and said, "Behold the blood of the covenant which the Lord

has made with you in accordance with all these words." (Exod. 24:6–8)

What was the significance of Moses' elaborate ritual? In the ancient Hebrew world, sharing sacrificial blood sealed a covenant between persons. This is what occurred when Moses splashed sacrificial blood first on the altar, which represented God, and then on the people: "The blood is especially vivid. Yahweh and the people are considered to be related by blood, for they have somehow shared the same blood in the rite."[70] On the downside, adds Dr. Scott Hahn, "the shed blood signified a solemn curse that Israel placed itself under by swearing the covenant oath. Through this ritual, in effect, Israel declared to God, 'Amen, we will share family life with you; you will be our Father, we will be your sons — or else we'll be damned!'"[71]

God told Moses that he would make Israel not only a "holy nation," but also a "kingdom of priests" (Exod. 19:6). Then Moses consecrated Israel — apparently as a nation[72] of priests — with the covenant-sealing ceremony described in Exodus 24. In Leviticus 8, Moses ordained Aaron and his sons as priests by sprinkling sacrificial blood on them and their priestly garments (8:30). The similarity between the blood sprinkling rituals of Leviticus 8 and Exodus 24 provides further biblical support that Moses apparently consecrated Israel as a nation of priests. Whether

[70] Dennis J. McCarthy, S.J., *Treaty and Covenant* (Rome: Pontifical Biblical Institute, 1963), 173. See Roland de Vaux, O.P., *The Early History of Israel* (Philadelphia: Westminster Press, 1978), 447.

[71] Scott Hahn, *A Father Who Keeps His Promises: God's Covenant Love in Scripture* (Ann Arbor, MI: Servant Publications, 1998), 150.

[72] Israel would not become a kingdom until later in salvation history.

or not Exodus 24 contains an ordination ceremony, Scripture makes clear that God called Israel to serve as a kingdom of priests (see Exod. 19:3–6). As a kingdom of priests, God intended Israel to play a priestly role on an international level, serving as an intermediary between himself and the nations.[73] Israel would not fulfill this role under the Old Covenant, and even within Israel the role of ministerial priesthood became restricted to the Levites following the people's worship of the golden calf (see Exod. 32). In any event, the covenant ritual at Sinai is unique in the Old Testament, for only here is an *entire people* "sprinkled with the blood and thereby consecrated to God in a special covenant."[74]

After the covenant was sealed, Moses, Aaron, Nadab, and Abihu ascended Sinai with seventy of Israel's elders for a celebratory communion meal: "[T]hey beheld God, and ate and drank" (Exod. 24:11). Hahn notes the significance of this and other Old Covenant communion meals and how they prefigure that of the New:

> From the ancient Hebrew perspective, covenant meals like this conveyed a twofold symbolic meaning: of the intimate family ties between covenant parties, and the awesome responsibilities that both parties assumed. The meal was a sign of the covenant blessing of communion, while the sacrificial victims signified the covenant curse that would befall Israel if they went back on their sworn oath. A similar twofold meaning is also present in the Holy

[73] Scott W. Hahn, *Kinship by Covenant: A Biblical Theological Study of Covenant Types and Texts in the Old and New Testaments* (Ann Arbor, MI: UM(Dissertation Services, 1996), 220–225.

[74] Léon-Dufour, *Sharing the Eucharistic Bread*, 145, 353, n. 26.

Eucharist, which Jesus instituted to be the sign of the New Covenant—as both a sacrifice and a meal—[and] which the Passover and the Sinai covenant both foreshadow (see 1 Cor. 10:1–22; 11:26–32).[75]

In summary, Israel's union with God was forged in a visible, tangible, sacramental way, with sacrifices and ceremonies and the eating of a communion meal. Charitably stated, Israelites were not united with God individually by simply praying an Old Covenant version of "The Sinner's Prayer." Israel was united with God collectively and in a sacramental manner, setting the unitive standard that Jesus would employ and advance in the New Covenant.

The New Moses: Jesus Shows the Way to the Eternal Promised Land

As Moses led Israel out of the bondage of slavery, Jesus came to liberate Israel and the world from enslavement to sin. As the Son of God and the Second Person of the Trinity, Jesus represented the ultimate confidant of God and mediator for the people. He did not simply advance himself as the chief teacher and governing authority in the New Covenant; he proclaimed himself as "the way, and the truth, and the life" (John 14:6).

Jesus deliberately chose *twelve* disciples. He intended to reconstitute the twelve tribes of Israel and thus the nation and kingdom of Israel (see CCC 877; 1 Pet. 2:9–10; Exod. 19:5–6). While Israel had never ceased to exist, Israel had been without a Davidic king since the fall of Solomon's Temple in the sixth century B.C. Jesus was the new king, the King of kings, who

---

[75] Hahn, *A Father Who Keeps His Promises*, 150. See CCC 1094–1096.

would reestablish Israel as an everlasting Kingdom of heaven, his Church (see Matt. 16:18–19).[76] The twelve apostles would serve as the foundation for that Kingdom (see Eph. 2:19–22), so Jesus gathered them together for the Last Supper to inaugurate the New Covenant. Jesus had not forgotten his Father's plan to make Israel a kingdom of priests to mediate his covenant to the nations, a plan unfulfilled in the Old Covenant but incorporated in modified form in the New. Jesus understood that "salvation is from the Jews" (John 4:22), so he also knew that he had to restore Israel before it could make disciples of all the nations (see Matt. 28:18–20).

Like the Old Covenant, the New Covenant would be sealed with blood. As the mediator for all mankind, Jesus served not only as a priest but also as a victim. There would be no need for the blood of animal sacrifices, for he would be the Lamb of God, who takes away the sin of the world. In addressing the Twelve at the Last Supper, Jesus speaks of his impending death on Calvary yet mysteriously offers his Body and Blood in advance, saying, "[T]his is my blood of the covenant" (Matt. 26:28). For the apostles, Jesus' words surely would have evoked memories of the Sinai covenant that their ancestors had made with God—except that Jesus was not renewing the Old Covenant; rather, he said that "this is the new covenant in my blood" (Luke 22:20). Outside of the Letter to the Hebrews, the words *blood* and *covenant* are used

---

[76] For a good overview on the biblical basis of the Church, read Catholics United for the Faith's (CUF) two free FAITH FACTS on the matter: "Rock Solid: Salvation History of the Church" and "That They May All Be One: The Difference the Church Makes." They are available online at http://www.cuf.org or by calling CUF toll-free at (800) MY-FAITH (693-2484).

together in the New Testament only regarding the institution of the Eucharist.[77]

To ratify the Old Covenant, Israel was covered with the blood of animals. To begin the New Covenant's ratification, Jesus gave his apostles his *own* blood to *drink* (see CCC 2806). In chapter 10, we will examine how Jesus could modify the Israelite ban on drinking sacrificial blood (see Lev. 17:10–14). Suffice it to say for now that the New Covenant would be a much more intimate relationship with God, one in which the restored kingdom of Israel would receive the eternal Son of God's very life by partaking of his Body and Blood. In addition, unlike the Sinai ratification, which took place only once in history, Jesus commanded his apostles to renew his covenant on a regular basis. Because of the infinite value of his Sacrifice, which logically flows from his being a divine Person, Jesus would have to die only once for all. However, because his Sacrifice culminated in everlasting glory at his Ascension, his apostles could re-present it again and again in memory of him. In this light, we are reminded that the Last Supper also fulfills and carries on the work of the annual Passover celebration of the Old Covenant.

---

[77] Matt. 26:28; Mark 14:24; Luke 22:20; 1 Cor. 11:25. The Letter to the Hebrews uses the words in tandem in Hebrews 9:18–21 to recall the Sinai covenant's ratification, and then later in 10:29 and 13:20 to refer to Christ's own redemptive act. The Letter to the Hebrews does not make explicit reference to the Sacrament of the Eucharist but rather focuses on the Calvary event from which the sacrament draws its value. To appreciate better the close connection between Matthew's account of the Last Supper and the Letter to the Hebrews' treatment of Christ's Sacrifice, see Albert Vanhoye, S.J., *Old Testament Priests and the New Priest: According to the New Testament*, trans. J. Bernard Orchard, O.S.B. (Petersham, MA: St. Bede's Publications, 1986), 202, 211, n. 58.

In establishing his New Covenant, Jesus thus ordained the apostles as his first priests, enabling them to partake in a more intimate blood ritual than their ancestors at Sinai. Protestant apologists argue that the Bible never uses the word *priest*—*kohen* (Hebrew) and *hiereus* (Greek)—to refer to anyone but Old Covenant priests and Jesus himself.[78] (Jesus does not explicitly refer to himself as a priest, but the Letter to the Hebrews, for example, does.) If Jesus really established New Covenant priests in addition to himself, they argue, why is the term not applied even to his apostles?

The New Testament does allude to the common priesthood of the faithful (1 Pet. 2:9, see Exod. 19:5–6), but in terms of offering sacrifices, that is, a ministerial priesthood, the apostles and others—for whatever reason—are not called priests. However, the New Testament does refer in Greek to bishops (*episkopoi*), presbyters (*presbuteroi*[79]) and deacons (*diakonoi*), which by the beginning of the early second century had become distinct, hierarchical offices. And, as St. Ignatius of Antioch conveys around A.D. 110, bishops and those they designated (presbyters) offered the Sacrifice of the Eucharist,[80] which Ignatius taught is "the Flesh of our Savior Jesus Christ, Flesh which suffered for our sins and which the Father, in His goodness, raised up again."[81]

---

[78] Actually, in discussing his ministering to the Gentiles in the "priestly service of the gospel of God," St. Paul uses the adjectival form (*priestly*) of *hiereus* (*hierouogounta*) in Romans 15:16.

[79] *Presbuteroi* also translates as "elders," and the English word *priests* is a contraction of *presbuteroi*.

[80] St. Ignatius of Antioch, *Letter to the Smyrnaeans*, 8, 1, as cited in William A. Jurgens, *The Faith of the Early Fathers* (Collegeville, MN.: Liturgical Press, 1970), no. 65, 1:25.

[81] Ibid., 7, 1, as cited in Jurgens, *Faith of the Early Fathers*, no. 64, 1:25.

Scripture also makes clear that early Church leaders performed the quintessential priestly ministry: offering sacrifices (see Heb. 8:3). The setting at the Last Supper, for example, is clearly a liturgical atmosphere. Christ and his apostles are celebrating the Passover but in a new way. And the Sacrifice that Christ pre-presents and anticipates is not for him alone to offer. Christ tells his apostles to continue his new Passover — this "new covenant in my blood" (Luke 22:20) — as a "remembrance" of him (Luke 22:19). He commands them to continue this new rite by sharing in his Melchizedekian priesthood, offering his one Sacrifice under the appearances of bread and wine as he first did at that first Last Supper (CCC 1337; see 611, 859, 1323, 1329–1330, 1333, 1350, 1541–1545).

If Israel were going to fulfill its mission as a kingdom of priests, of making disciples of all the nations, there would have to be priests to minister to the nations. After Christ and because of Christ, the apostles would be the first priests to provide that "pure offering" among the Gentiles that Malachi prophesied (Mal. 1:11; see CCC 1350), a Sacrifice that would unite the Gentiles as the Body of Christ, as Paul affirms (see 1 Cor. 10:14–22). In summary, both in Scripture and in other writings, the early Church affirmed the sacrificial nature of the Eucharist and thus the priesthood of the apostles and their successors, a subject that will be addressed in more detail in chapter 13.

Although the apostles would minister on earth, their priesthood, as with Christ's, is not of this earth (see Heb. 8:4). The apostles and ministerial priests thereafter would serve *in persona Christi*, in the person and power of Jesus Christ, the high priest of the New Covenant who ministers in everlasting glory in the heavenly sanctuary (see Heb. 8:3–7 and CCC 1548). The ministry of New Covenant priests would also include forgiving the faithful's ongoing sins in the sacrament of Reconciliation by applying the merits of Christ's one Sacrifice (see John 20:19–23).

Finally, Jesus not only offered a Sacrifice to inaugurate the New Covenant; he instituted a communion sacrifice, which his followers would not only re-present but also partake of in memory of him. Here again Jesus fulfills both the Sinai covenant and the Passover sacrifice in instituting the Eucharistic Sacrifice, a Sacrifice that the Church not only offers in celebrating Mass but of which the faithful also partake. Jesus came to establish definitive and permanent communion between man and God. Indeed, Jesus tells his disciples that by offering and partaking of his Sacrifice, they can live forever (see John 6:51–58).

Present among His People, Atoning for Our Sins

When a couple gets married, they typically assume a more intimate living arrangement. The covenant made at Sinai between God and Israel was no different. Israel could not ascend to heaven — not yet at least — so the transcendent God had to condescend to or accommodate his beloved Israel. The marital imagery is not inappropriate because, on many occasions, Yahweh described Israel as his bride — and also as an adulteress when she went astray. To dwell more intimately with his newly espoused Israel, God summoned Moses again to the summit of Sinai, instructing him to build a tabernacle, the details of which are given in Exodus 25–31. The tabernacle, or "tent of meeting," served as an ongoing sign of God's presence as Israel traveled through the wilderness to the Promised Land, and it was eventually replaced by the more ornate Temple once Israel reached the Promised Land (see 1 Kings 6–10).

Recall that the tabernacle and the Temple each consisted of an outer courtyard, an inner holy place, and an innermost holy of holies, or most holy place. The furnishings of the holy place included the altar of incense, a lampstand and the table with the "bread of the Presence," or "shewbread" (Exod. 25:30), that is, the twelve loaves of bread that represented the twelve tribes of Israel.[82] But during the Old Covenant, Yahweh was most intimately present on earth in the most holy place, his mercy seat positioned atop the Ark of the Covenant and flanked by two angels (Exod. 25:8, 17–22).

Today's Catholic churches in the New Covenant also possess a special presence of the divine. Jesus Christ remains omnipresent, that is, existing everywhere as a divine Person, but, in the tabernacles of Catholic churches throughout the world, he is uniquely and miraculously present — Body, Blood, Soul, and Divinity — in the Eucharist. Because Jesus' one Sacrifice is regularly re-presented in the Mass on a church's main altar, which is located in the sanctuary, and because tabernacles are

---

[82] Dr. Margaret Barker notes, "The extreme holiness of the Shewbread is confirmed by the fact that when the desert tabernacle was moved, the ark and the table of Shewbread were the only items to have three covers (Num. 4:5–8)" (Barker, "The Temple Roots of the Liturgy"). In Hebrew, the shewbread is literally *lehem panim* — that is, "bread of the face" or "bread of the presence" (Exod. 30:25). Barker notes that *panim* was used as a circumlocution for the Lord himself. "Perhaps this is how 'Bread of Presence' should be understood," concludes Barker. "It would certainly explain the great holiness of the Shewbread and the special status of the table on which it rested." The shewbread is seen as a prefigurement of the Eucharist, which is the "Bread of Life" that is both eaten and known as the Real Presence, residing in the New Covenant analogue to the Temple: tabernacles located within church sanctuaries.

often also located in a church's sanctuary, the sanctuary is the most sacred space in a church, serving as the New Covenant analogue to the most holy place in the ancient Temple.

In the Old Covenant, as we have noted, only the high priest could enter the most holy place, and then only once a year on the Day of Atonement (see Lev. 16). If he attempted to draw near to the mercy seat on any other day, he would die (Lev. 16:1–2), as would any other Israelite who attempted to usurp his high priestly role (Num. 3:10; 8:7). Through his definitive Sacrifice, Jesus tore down the barrier of sin between God and man, symbolized by the rending of the Temple curtain (Matt. 27:51) when he completed his suffering on Calvary for us (see John 19:30). Now we can not only draw near to God through Baptism in becoming temples of the Holy Spirit (see 1 Cor. 6:19) and worshipping the Eucharistic Christ in the tabernacle, but we can draw even nearer by actually partaking of him in the Eucharist!

In the New Covenant, the faithful can also suffer death — a more serious spiritual one — if they draw near to the Eucharist and partake of our Lord in an unworthy manner (see 1 Cor. 11:27–30; CCC 1385, 1861). But Christ came so that we might live, not die (see John 3:16). Christ's action on Calvary signifies the extent of God's love for Israel *and* for the whole world. Whereas the Old Covenant sacrifices signified the punishment Israel would face if it violated its sacred oath to God, the New Covenant Sacrifice exemplifies the Self-Sacrifice God was willing to make even though Israel had egregiously failed in keeping its covenant oath. God not only demonstrates fidelity in sticking with unfaithful Israel, but he also manifests his unfathomable love in taking on the sins of Israel and the whole world so that we might be spared everlasting punishment.

God Draws Near to His People

Offering It Every Day:
The Tamid Sets the Stage for the Lamb of God

In addition to housing God's special presence, the Old Testament tabernacle provided a place at which Israel could offer sacrifices. One of the most significant sacrifices in prefiguring Christ's Sacrifice on Calvary and its re-presentation in the Mass was the twice-daily sacrifice of lambs known as the Tamid ("continual") offering. While providing various liturgical directives atop Mount Sinai, God instructed Moses to institute the Tamid:

> Now this is what you shall offer upon the altar: two lambs a year old day by day continually. One lamb you shall offer in the morning, and the other lamb you shall offer in the evening;... It shall be a continual burnt offering throughout your generations at the door of the tent of meeting before the Lord, where I will meet you, to speak there to you. There I will meet with the people of Israel, and it shall be sanctified by my glory. (Exod. 29:38–39, 42–43).

As a burnt offering, the Tamid was intended, in some sense, to make atonement for Israel (see Lev. 1:3–13), so that communion with God could be restored or renewed. A burnt offering would also consume the whole sacrifice, prefiguring Christ's total Self-Offering. In addition, to the Catholic mind, the offering of grain and wine along with the Tamid lambs (Exod. 29:40–45) might evoke images of the Lamb of God's being later offered under the appearances of bread and wine at Mass.

There is a basis for such liturgical anticipation. In offering the Tamid, Israel recalled the "unfinished business" of the Aqedah, the sacrifice of Isaac in Genesis 22. God praised Abraham for his faithfulness and said that he would one day provide a

Lamb on that mountain (Moriah), a lamb that Abraham and his Hebrew descendants understood would bring about a universal blessing. For the Israelites, who focused particularly on Isaac's heroic self-sacrifice, the Aqedah was not simply a past event to be recalled, but a future pledge of divine blessing. In general, as an ancient rabbinical commentary notes, Israel's lamb offerings were offered in light of the Aqedah: "The lamb was chosen so as to recall the merit of the Unique man [Isaac] who was bound upon one of the mountains like a lamb of sacrifice on the altar."[83]

The Tamid stood out as a special "remembrance" of the Aqedah:

> When Abraham our father bound Isaac his Son, the Holy One, blessed be He, instituted [the sacrifice of] two lambs [that is, the Tamid], one in the morning, and the other in the evening. What is the purpose of this? It is in order that when Israel offers the perpetual [Tamid] sacrifice upon the altar ... the Holy One, blessed be He, may remember the Binding of Isaac.[84]

The Tamid served as a daily reminder to Israel that God would yet one day provide a special lamb on Moriah. In addition, the Tamid also recalled the Passover sacrifice, for in offering the

---

[83] Marginal gloss on Targum Neofiti to Leviticus 22:27, as cited in Robert Hayward, "The Present State of Research into the Targumic Account of the Sacrifice of Isaac," 139.

[84] *Lev. Rabbah* 2:7, as cited in and translated by Geza Vermes, "Redemption and Genesis XXII," *Scripture and Tradition in Judaism: Haggadic Studies*, 2nd ed. (Leiden, Neth.: Brill, 1973), 209. Leviticus Rabbah is part of the Jewish Midrash (see page 69, n. 38 for information on the Midrash). *Leviticus Rabbah* was written in the early Christian centuries.

Tamid "they shall know that I brought them out of the land of Egypt that I might dwell among them; I am the Lord their God" (Exod. 29:46). In turn, as noted in chapter 6, a well-known rabbinic commentary written after the time of Christ linked the Aqedah and Passover: "And when I see the blood [of the Passover lamb], I will pass over you (Ex 12:13) — [for] I see the blood of Isaac's Aqedah."[85] The implication is that, as the Passover lamb's blood delivered Israel from slavery, and the Tamid served as a daily offering for atonement, the universal fulfillment of the Aqedah would come through the blood of the lamb that God would provide on Mount Moriah. As also noted in chapter 6, the "Poem of the Four Nights" prophesied that Israel and the world would one day be redeemed on Passover night.[86]

The blood of Jesus, the Lamb of God, would provide that universal redemption through his Sacrifice of Calvary, fulfilling the Aqedah, Tamid, and Passover sacrifices. In addition, the perfected work of the Tamid would continue in Masses thereafter, the ongoing application of the merits of Christ's Sacrifice being made present for the ongoing reconciliation of the faithful with God.[87]

---

[85] *Mekhilta de Rabbi Ishmael*, Pisha 7, lines 78–79, as cited in Hayward, "The Present State of Research into the Targumic Account of the Sacrifice of Isaac," 140. *Mekhilta de Rabbi Ishmael* is also part of the Jewish Midrash. As indicated earlier, the *Mekhilta* was written in the early Christian centuries.

[86] Hayward, "The Present State of Research into the Targumic Account of the Sacrifice of Isaac," 140.

[87] One might argue that, as Isaac's Aqedah was remembered through the daily Tamid lamb offerings until Christ's first coming and the establishment of his Kingdom, the remembrance of the Eucharistic Sacrifice perfects the Aqedah, making present Christ's one Sacrifice until the consummation of that same Kingdom at

The Biblical Roots of the Mass

An Atoning Sacrifice

The Day of Atonement sacrifices, described in Leviticus 16:1–34, shed further light on how Christ would redeem the world. Each year the high priest would offer a bull to atone for his own sins and two goats for Israel's sins. He would apply the blood of the bull and one goat—sin offerings—to Yahweh's mercy seat in the most holy place. The high priest would offer the other goat—also a sin offering—by imposing his hands on it, yet without killing the goat (Lev. 16:10, 20–22). The goat would thereby symbolically take on the sins of the people and carry them away into the wilderness. (The term *scapegoat*, meaning one who conveniently "bears the blame of others," derives from the second goat of this ancient ritual.) The high priest would further offer a burnt offering for himself and also one for the people on the Day of Atonement (Lev. 16:3, 5, 24).

Christ's Second Coming. Geza Vermes elaborates on the connection between the Aqedah, Passover, and Tamid sacrifices with Christ's Offering in the Eucharist: "According to [Aqedah theology], remission of sin, as well as present and future salvation, were due to the unique sacrifice of Isaac. The Passover was not only the annual commemoration of his sacrifice, but also a joyful reminder of its first decisive fruit and a prayer to God to bring about the final salvation of man. In addition, God's remembrance was not only sought yearly, in Nisan, but day by day in a perpetual [Tamid] sacrifice of lambs invoking His forgiveness, mercy and love. The frequent celebration of the Eucharistic meal may, therefore, be understood as the introduction into Christianity of this other element of the Akedah theology: the perpetual remembrance of the one perfect Sacrifice until the Kingdom comes" (Vermes, "Redemption and Genesis XXII," 226–227; *Akedah* is a variant spelling of *Aqedah*).

The sacrifices served a contemporary purpose while also pre-figuring the New Covenant. Goats and bulls were the images under which Egyptian demon gods were worshipped, a misguided spiritual worship the Israelites had assimilated during their four hundred years of enslavement in Egypt. For example, consider the golden-calf incident following God's giving of the Ten Com-mandments. The solution? Egyptian gods were to be sacrificed, not offered sacrifices in idolatrous worship.[88]

The repeated sacrifice of bulls and goats on the Day of Atone-ment indicated their inability to atone satisfactorily for Israel's sins and that this ordinance forever (Lev. 16:29), like that of the Passover celebration, would one day be transformed, "for it is impossible that the blood of bulls and goats should take away sins" (Heb. 10:4). Could someone fulfill both ordinances, simultaneously serving as the Passover lamb of God, who delivers us from the bondage of sin and Satan, and the scapegoat who atones for our sins?

The prophet Jeremiah affirmed that it would take a "new cov-enant," a covenant better than the one initiated after the Exodus from Egypt, for God to remember Israel's sins "no more" (Jer. 31:31–34). Complementing Jeremiah's new covenant prophecy, the prophet Isaiah taught that a suffering-servant lamb (Isa. 53:7) would deliver Israel from sin. The prophet recalls the Exodus from Egypt (52:3–4) and then says that God will redeem Is-rael (Jerusalem) in a new and greater Exodus (52:7–12), one in which "all the ends of the earth shall see the salvation of our God" (52:10).

This suffering-servant lamb would also perfect the scapegoat typology of the Day of Atonement sacrifices. For he would be

---

[88] See page 66, n. 37.

"despised and rejected by men" and yet triumphant because, although "wounded for our transgressions" and "bruised for our iniquities," by "his stripes" we would be healed (Isa. 53:3, 5). He would be like a "lamb that is led to the slaughter" (53:7) and yet serve as both priest and victim, because he would bear "the sin of many" (53:12), making "himself an offering for sin" (53:10).

This lamb, this scapegoat, could be no mere human. No one—not Moses, not any of the prophets, not any of the kings of Israel nor any other Israelite—had ever even *claimed* that he could offer his life as an effective sin offering for Israel or the whole world, let alone attempted it. Despite the Israelites' wilderness tabernacle and Temple, despite their kingdom, despite all of their daily and annual sacrifices, they had never been truly liberated from their worst enemy—sin. Israel knew that the suffering servant would have to be a truly remarkable person.

What person could suffer once and redeem us from our sins (Day of Atonement) yet perhaps have his one sacrifice regularly commemorated in a distinct way, a way that would continue to carry out the work of redemption (see CCC 1364) and, at the same time, perfect the ordinance forever of the Passover sacrifice and also, possibly, the continual offering of the Tamid sacrifice? Who indeed? As the Old Covenant drew to a close, the Messiah prepared to come to answer all of the questions.

Questions for Reflection and Discussion

1. Compare and contrast the covenant-ratification ceremonies of the Old and New Covenants. (a) Who were the mediators in each, and how was Israel represented? (b) Why was and is "the blood of the covenant" such an important feature of these ceremonies? (c) How was the covenant sealed with blood for

those in the Old Covenant versus those in the New Covenant? Does the manner suggest a greater intimacy with God in the New? Explain. (d) What was the "downside" of the blood of the covenant and the communion meals in the Old and New Covenants? (e) Yet what does the New Covenant show forth about God's disposition toward mankind?

2. Explain how God unifies Israel in a corporate and sacramental way in both the Old and New Covenants. In light of this evidence, and the evidence regarding the Lord's Supper considered in the last chapter, can we infer any biblical lessons about Catholic and Protestant views of salvation?

3. Jesus ordained the apostles at the Last Supper. Yet their priesthood is rooted in heaven, not earth. In light of Hebrews 8:3–7 and what we have learned in this and previous chapters, explain the difference between the Levitical and Melchizedekian priesthoods.

4. How would you respond to a Christian who asserted that the New Testament alludes to a priesthood of all believers, but not New Covenant priests who offer sacrifices?

5. What basic similarities can you see between the Old Covenant tabernacle/Temple and New Covenant churches?

6. (a) How did the Tamid sacrifice prefigure the Mass? (b) How did the sacrifices of the Aqedah and Passover as well as the "Poem of the Four Nights" factor into this prefiguration? (c) Considering that the Tamid was offered in both the morning and the evening, can another Eucharistic parallel be drawn in light of the pure offering that Malachi says would be offered by the Gentiles, that is, "the nations" (Mal. 1)? Explain.

7. (a) Where do we get the term *scapegoat*? (b) The Day of Atonement was for the atonement of sins. Yet, according to Jeremiah (31:31–34), a "new covenant" would forgive sins in a more significant manner. How is the suffering servant discussed in Isaiah 52:13–53:12 related to this new covenant? If the suffering servant is indeed to fulfill this new covenant, how does this scriptural passage convey that he will do so? Who might this suffering servant be?

8. (a) Why did high priests in the Old Covenant have to enter the tabernacle / Temple sanctuary every year, whereas Jesus had to enter the heavenly sanctuary only once? (See Heb. 7:26–28; 9:11–14, 23–28; 10:1–4.) (b) How can we biblically argue that Jesus remains in the heavenly sanctuary, continuing to serve as a priest, yet also is present elsewhere? (c) Jesus' Sacrifice of Calvary brought together and fulfilled simultaneously the Day of Atonement, Passover, and Tamid sacrifices. How does Jesus' ongoing ministry in the celebration of the Mass continue the work of these respective, fulfilled sacrifices?

Part 3

Mass Appeal
Living on the Lamb

10

Man Shall Live Forever
on This Bread Alone

Jesus Announces the Eucharist

Background Reading
    1 Kings 17:8–16
    1 Kings 19:4–8
    Exodus 16:1–36
    2 Kings 4:42–44
    John 6:1–7:I
    Leviticus 17:10–14

Israel had long anticipated that a descendant of David would be the Messiah, that is, "the Christ" or "anointed one" who would restore their kingdom (see Jer. 23:5–6). Scripture foretold that the Messiah would come from Bethlehem, which in Hebrew means "House of Bread" (Mic. 5:2), a fitting birthplace for the One who would become known as the Bread of Life. "Do not be afraid," the angel Gabriel told Mary, saying that she would bear a son named Jesus, a name that means "Yahweh saves" (Luke 1:30–31; see CCC 430). "[T]he Lord will give to him the throne of his father David," Gabriel added, "and he will reign over the house of Jacob for ever, and of his kingdom there will be no end" (Luke 1:32–33; see 2 Sam. 7:8–16; Matt. 1:1).

An angel also reassured Joseph that his wife was carrying a child who would "save his people from their sins" (Matt. 1:20–21), and an angel also affirmed at Jesus' birth that the Christ had been born (Luke 2:11). Thirty years later, John the Baptist clarified that the Messiah had come not just to save Israel, but to serve as "the Lamb of God, who takes away the sin of the world" (John 1:29).

When John proclaimed Jesus "the Lamb of God," little did the Israelites realize that they would one day soon have the opportunity to partake of this divine Lamb. They recognized Jesus as a prospective Messiah, one who would somehow restore the kingdom of Israel, but they did not grasp that his victory would be over sin and death, not political rulers (see John 6:14–15). Even the twelve apostles did not initially grasp that he was the new Passover Lamb and that, as such, he would not only die, but also become a meal, just as the long-standing Passover precepts directed regarding the lambs sacrificed.

Eating Jesus! Many of his shocked disciples chose not to follow Christ further when he announced, "[H]e who eats my flesh and drinks my blood has eternal life, and I will raise him up at the last day. For my flesh is food indeed, and my blood is drink indeed" (John 6:54–55). Jesus' famous Bread of Life discourse is the focus of this chapter. But consider initially the revulsion the Israelites had at the thought of consuming Christ's body and blood. God had strictly prohibited the Jews from drinking the blood of sacrificed animals (see Gen. 9:4; Lev. 17:10–14), let alone the blood of human beings. As will be discussed later in this chapter, this divine prohibition constituted the major stumbling block for many Jews' acceptance of Christ's words about the Eucharist.

In addition, in more recent times, the Church has confronted other objections about the Eucharist, including from some Christians. Christians agree that Jesus was a charismatic prophet who performed extraordinary miracles, yet some who do not accept the Eucharist seem to forget that he is first and foremost a divine person, One for whom all things are possible. They seem to focus rather on Christ's limited human nature. How can everyone eat and drink Jesus? How can one man's body feed so many people? In the traditional Passover, many lambs had to be sacrificed to nourish the Jewish multitudes, but, respectfully stated, these Christians might assert, there does not appear to be enough of Jesus to go around. In John 6, they might note, Jesus does make comparisons between himself and the manna that the ancient Israelites ate every day while journeying to their earthly Promised Land. But, they might add, we surely cannot understand our Lord to be saying that we would somehow consume him on a regular basis.

Bread in Blessed Abundance:
Prefiguring the Bread of Life

Although Jesus' words certainly seem puzzling even to many modern Christians uninformed by a Catholic perspective, the miracle of the Eucharist does have biblical precedents. The miraculous multiplication of food in the Old Covenant sets the stage for something even more astonishing in the New. Consider first the widow of Zarephath, whom God had destined to provide food for his prophet Elijah (1 Kings 17:8–16). When Elijah asked the widow to bring some bread and water, the poor woman told him she had only enough flour and oil to make one more meal for herself and her son, after which they would die of starvation. Elijah told the woman not to fear, "for thus says the Lord the

God of Israel, 'The jar of meal shall not be spent, and the cruse of oil shall not fail, until the day that the Lord sends rain upon the earth.'" The widow believed Elijah and was blessed: "And she went and did as Elijah said; and she, and he, and her household ate for many days. The jar of meal was not spent, neither did the cruse of oil fail, according to the word of the Lord which he spoke by Elijah" (1 Kings 17:4–16).

The Catholic Church teaches that several other Old Testament readings prefigure the Eucharist. Most notable are three readings paired with Gospel readings from John 6 in Year B of the Church's Sunday cycle of readings. They are read on the Seventeenth, Eighteenth and Nineteenth Sundays of Ordinary Time, which fall during the summer.[89]

On the Eighteenth Sunday, we read about the manna that God sent the Israelites in the wilderness when the nation feared death (Exod. 16:2–4, 12–15). The manna sustained them each day as they journeyed to the Promised Land, much like the Eucharist sustains us on our pilgrimage to heaven, the eternal Promised Land. Although not noted in the excerpted Mass reading, the book of Exodus makes clear that God provided sufficient manna for every household. On the Nineteenth Sunday, we read about how Elijah, weary from a one-day sojourn in the desert, sat

---

[89] In cycle B, the Church reads from John 6 on five consecutive Sundays (the Seventeenth to Twenty-First Sundays of Ordinary Time). Eucharistic connections are also made with the Old Testament readings provided on the Twentieth and Twenty-First Sundays. On the Twentieth Sunday, Proverbs 9:1–6 speaks of Wisdom providing food to eat and wine to drink, and on the Twenty-First Sunday an allusion is made in Joshua (24:1–2, 15–17, 18) to the miraculous manna God provided to sustain the Israelites in the wilderness.

down and prayed for death (1 Kings 19:4–8). However, miraculously sustained by a cake and water that an angel subsequently provided him, the prophet continued his journey in the desert for forty days and forty nights until he reached Mount Horeb.

Second Kings 4:42–44, read on the Seventeenth Sunday, records perhaps the most remarkable event in the Old Testament that prefigures the Eucharist. The prophet Elisha, Elijah's successor, miraculously multiplied a small number of loaves and a sack of grain:

> A man came from Baal-shalishah, bringing the man of God [Elisha] bread of the first fruits, twenty loaves of barley, and fresh ears of grain in his sack. And Elisha said, "Give to the men, that they may eat." But his servant said, "How am I to set this before a hundred men?" So he repeated, "Give them to the men, that they may eat, for thus says the LORD, 'They shall eat and have some left.'" So he set it before them. And they ate, and had some left, according to the word of the LORD.

Some scholars might argue that Elisha's servant persuaded everyone to ration sacrificially the limited amount of food. But the text gives no hint of such cooperation. The text recognizes the incredulity of Elisha's servant and then simply notes that all of the men ate with some left over. No natural explanation is provided for the abundance; rather, a miracle is implied because it was accomplished "according to the word of the LORD." In all three of these Sunday readings from Year B, God demonstrates that miraculously providing abundant bread is certainly not beyond his omnipotent power over the laws of physics. He calls his people to believe that he can provide abundantly from seemingly meager resources.

"What Are They among So Many?"

Jesus calls his closest disciples to a similar faith in using five loaves and two fish to feed five thousand men and an unspecified number of women and children who had gathered to hear him preach (see Matt. 13:21). Apart from the Resurrection, this is the only miracle that all four Gospels report (see Matt. 14:13–21; Mark 6:32–44; Luke 9:10–17; John 6:1–14). John perceptively notes in his account that Passover was at hand (John 6:4), an appropriate time for Jesus to teach the Jews that they would one day eat his Body. But first he would multiply loaves to give them "a taste" of how he would nourish them all.

Many non-Catholic Christians agree with the Church that Jesus performed a miracle in multiplying the loaves and fish (see CCC 1335), but they believe that Jesus spoke only figuratively about consuming his Body and Blood later in John 6. The Eucharist for them is only symbolic.

We see in John 6 that Jesus' first disciples did not anticipate his multiplication of loaves. With the great crowd assembled, Jesus tested Philip, asking him how it would be possible to buy enough bread for the thousands of people to eat. Philip said that "two hundred denarii," that is, two hundred times the daily wage for a laborer, would not be enough for each person to get a meager ration (John 6:7). Andrew, Peter's brother, then told Jesus in words similar to those of Elisha's servant, "There is a lad here who has five barley loaves and two fish; but what are they among so many?" (John 6:8–9; see 2 Kings 4:43).

Jesus directed his disciples to have the crowd sit down, and then he blessed the loaves and fish. The crowd ate their fill of both bread and fish and the disciples filled twelve baskets with leftover fragments from the original five barley loaves (John 6:10–13).

The miracle evoked the memory of Moses, another great Israelite who had provided much food for many people. Having witnessed the miracle, the crowd proclaimed, "This is indeed the prophet who is to come into the world!" (John 6:14), a reference to Moses' prophecy that God would one day raise up a prophet like him (Deut. 18:15). Moses was a lawgiver, providing the Ten Commandments, while Jesus both reiterated and advanced the Decalogue with his Sermon on the Mount (Matt. 5–7). Moses served as mediator of the Old Covenant, and Jesus came to mediate the New Covenant. Moses liberated Israel from bondage to man, and Jesus would liberate mankind from bondage to sin. Finally, Moses prayed down manna from heaven; now it was Jesus' turn to feed the multitudes.

After feeding the five thousand near the Sea of Galilee, Jesus attempted to nourish the crowd in a different manner the following day in Capernaum, telling them to labor not for food that perishes but for that which endures unto eternal life. Jesus added that he himself would provide this food (John 6:27). When Jesus told the people that they must believe in him as one sent by God, they asked for a sign, noting that Moses, their great ancestral leader, had provided their fathers manna, "bread from heaven" (John 6:31; see Exod. 16:4).

Of course, God, not Moses, had provided the manna. More importantly, Jesus told the people that his Father, not Moses, provides the "*true* bread from heaven" that "gives life to the world" (John 6:32–33, emphasis added). Jesus shockingly added that *he* was that true bread and, causing further shock, indicated that he had come "not to do my own will, but the will of him who sent me" (John 6:38). In other words, Jesus was flatly stating that the God the Jewish people revered — the God of Abraham, Isaac, and Jacob — had actually sent him to serve them. (The shock of these statements would grow, as Jesus made clearer his role as "the bread from heaven.")

Previewing the New Passover?

The Jews murmured in disbelief, wondering how a mere man could come down from heaven. Instead of reassuring the people that he was just speaking figuratively, Jesus tested them further, noting that while their ancestors had eaten manna in the desert and died, those who eat his Bread will live forever, for "the bread which I shall give for the life of the world is my flesh" (John 6:51).

Scripture scholars, including non-Catholic ones, generally recognize the sacrificial nature of the passage,[90] for Jesus says that he would give his flesh for the world's benefit, implying, apparently, a sacrifice of his life. Jesus would eventually speak of his impending death more explicitly (see Matt. 16:21), but prior to the Bread of Life discourse, John the Baptist had implied Christ's Sacrifice in designating him as "the Lamb of God, who takes away the sin of the world." Recall also that John the Evangelist says that the great feast of Passover was at hand (John 6:4). Jesus seems to be making a subtle Passover point: as the Lamb of God, he would emulate his Passover predecessors, serving as both sacrifice and meal. Yet Jesus conveys that his Sacrifice would have much wider impact than the traditional Passover sacrifice — extending beyond Israel to the whole world — and also serve as a definitive offering. Believers would need no subsequent lambs

---

[90] W. Leonard, "The Gospel of Jesus Christ according to St. John," in Dom Bernard Orchard et al., eds., A Catholic Commentary on Holy Scripture (New York: Thomas Nelson and Sons, 1953), 993, no. 795b.

for sustenance, for partaking of Jesus alone would enable them to live forever in heaven, not simply gain liberation from Egyptian enslavement. Furthermore, a worldwide redemption resonates with the universal blessing that God had told Abraham he would one day provide.

The *Catechism* (no. 1355) also affirms the New Covenant Passover implications of John 6:51, citing it in a passage on the Mass:

> In the communion, preceded by the Lord's prayer and the breaking of the bread, the faithful receive "the bread of heaven" and "the cup of salvation," the body and blood of Christ who offered himself "for the life of the world." [John 6:51]

"They Shall Eat the Flesh": Perfecting Exodus 12:8

Jesus appears to hint at the sacrificial aspect of his impending Passover Sacrifice in John 6:51 and then focuses more attention on the communion-meal aspect of his Sacrifice during the rest of the Bread of Life discourse. The controversy surrounding the meal aspect of Christ's Sacrifice relates, in part, to language issues. Jesus principally spoke Aramaic, a Semitic language related to Hebrew, but the Gospel of John is written in Greek. Up to 6:51, John uses *esthio* to communicate what Christ meant by *eating*. While some argue that *esthio* can be understood figuratively as well as literally, the real issue is the context of John 6. The context of a passage best determines the meaning of a given word used. In other words, how do the Jewish people respond to his presentation? They understand him to be speaking literally, not figuratively: "The Jews then disputed among themselves, saying, 'How can this man give us his flesh to eat?'" (John 6:52).

Jesus does not allay their concern with a clarification; he becomes more explicit and emphatic in his language. To capture Christ's meaning, John uses *esthio* again in 6:53, but then switches in 6:54, 56, and 57 to *trogo* (to gnaw or chew), a more descriptive word for eating. As if to distinguish the inferior manna from Christ's life-giving flesh, John summarizes the Bread of Life discourse in 6:58: "This is the bread which came down from heaven, not such as the fathers ate [*esthio*] and died," said Jesus. "[H]e who eats [*trogo*] this bread will live for ever."[91]

Not surprisingly, the Jewish people gathered *continued* to understand Jesus literally about eating his flesh, but their concern had risen to the level of anxiety, and their allegiance to Christ was now in doubt: "Many of his disciples, when they heard it, said, 'This is a hard saying: who can listen to it?'" (John 6:61). Here again, Jesus does not provide reassurance to his disciples, who did not want to believe that they would actually have to eat his Flesh and drink his Blood:

> But Jesus, knowing in himself that his disciples murmured at it, said to them, "Do you take offense at this? Then what if you were to see the Son of man ascending where he was before? It is the spirit that gives life, the flesh is of no avail; the words that I have spoken to you are spirit and life. But there are some of you that do not believe." (John 6:61–64)

---

[91] See Paul R. McReynolds, *Word Study Greek-English New Testament* (Wheaton, IL: Tyndale House, 1998). 353–354. See also Spiros Zodhiates, ed., *The Hebrew-Greek Key Study Bible*, New American Standard Bible version (Chattanooga, TN: AMG Publishers, 1990, 1408; and 33, no. 2068, and 73, no. 5176 of the "Greek Dictionary of the New Testament," appendix.

Contrary to what some Christians think about this passage, Jesus does not move away from a literal understanding of his previous words. Rather, he appears to be providing a basis for how we can understand his foregoing literal words. Commentators have wrestled over the meaning of the words "It is the spirit that gives life, the flesh is of no avail." Some argue that Jesus is basically admonishing his disciples that a spiritual view would enable them by faith to believe in his Eucharistic Real Presence, whereas an unspiritual, carnal, "fleshly" perspective would be of no avail.[92]

I also suggest that Jesus is simply saying that his flesh, that is, his human nature *by itself*, has no power to give life, eternal or otherwise. However, when united to his divine Person by the Holy Spirit at his Incarnation, and, more significantly, when it becomes present as the Sacrifice of Calvary completed at Mass by the power of that same Spirit, it becomes a participant in wondrous divine blessing. St. Cyril of Alexandria argues similarly, equating "the spirit that quickeneth" with Christ's divinity, and "the flesh that profiteth nothing" with Christ's mere human nature on its own.[93]

In any event, Jesus' words did not reassure many of his followers, for "after this many of his disciples drew back and no longer went about with him" (John 6:66).

At this point, notice that Jesus did not turn to his twelve apostles and say, "Hey, guys, what's wrong with that crowd? They

---

[92] See, for example, Dom Ralph Russell, "St. John," in Rev. Reginald C. Fuller et al., eds., *A New Commentary on Holy Scripture*, rev. ed. (Nashville: Thomas Nelson Publishers, 1975), p. 1051, no. 808m.

[93] As cited in Leonard, "The Gospel of Jesus Christ," in *A Catholic Commentary on Holy Scripture*, 994, no. 795h.

completely misunderstood me about eating my body and drinking my blood! They thought I was speaking literally!" Jesus had cleared up misunderstandings among his disciples on other occasions, but not here. There was no reason. He had clearly stated his words about eating his Body and drinking his Blood, and his audience had clearly understood his words. Instead, Jesus turned to his closest disciples and asked them a direct, candid question:

> Jesus said to the twelve, "Will you also go away?" Simon Peter answered him, "Lord, to whom shall we go? You have the words of eternal life; and we have believed, and have come to know, that you are the Holy One of God." (John 6:67–69)

Yet some Christians insist that Christ meant his words figuratively, tipping his hand when he said that "it is the spirit that gives life, the flesh is of no avail; the words that I have spoken to you are spirit and life" (John 6:63). They infer that Jesus literally meant that his flesh could not be profitable and therefore his words in John 6 must be interpreted figuratively, that is, to "eat the body and drink the blood" of Christ simply means to do God's will, and that by heeding his words they will gain "spirit and life." Such an interpretation conflicts with the overwhelming contextual evidence, from Christ's repeated and emphatic words to his disciples' increasing aversion that concluded in their abandonment of him. If Jesus were simply clarifying that his flesh was truly useless and that he only meant a spiritual consumption of his words, you would expect Jesus to reassure the crowd unequivocally and that the mollified crowd would have subsequently remained. Nothing of the sort happened.

In addition, one must not impose on John 6 a figurative, latter-day meaning that is disconnected from a first-century Jewish worldview. To "eat the body and drink the blood," or, more simply, "to devour my flesh," was figuratively used as an ancient Hebrew idiom, but the meaning of the idiom does not help the case of those who argue against a literal interpretation of Jesus' words in John 6. The idiom denoted the violence of war, as illustrated most clearly in Psalm 27:2–3: "When evildoers come at me to devour my flesh, my foes and my enemies themselves stumble and fall. Though an army encamp against me, my heart will not fear; though war be waged upon me even then I will trust" (see Deut. 32:42, NAB). The RSVCE renders the passage in a similar manner: "When evildoers assail me, uttering slanders against me, my adversaries and foes, they shall stumble and fall" (Ps. 27:2). A footnote affirms the Hebrew idiom, explaining that what is translated as "uttering slanders against me" literally means "to eat up my flesh." To eat up someone's flesh, then, was a figurative way of saying you wanted to destroy or kill that person, or at least destroy his reputation through slander.

Consequently, if we insert a figurative meaning into John 6:54 that accurately represents the ancient Hebrew language, the passage is reduced to nonsense. Jesus is made to look like a demented, pious masochist or a crazed demoniac: "He who kills me [or slanders me] has eternal life." The Jewish crowd in Capernaum that day would have been aware of this Hebrew idiom and thus would have understood how foolish Jesus would have sounded had he intended his words figuratively. The crowd had difficulty with Jesus not because they thought he was misusing a Hebrew idiom, but rather precisely because they understood him to be speaking literally. Indeed, the text of John 6 conveys that the crowd responded to Jesus as if he *were* speaking literally, and, for his part, Jesus said and did everything to reinforce a literal understanding among all those gathered.

The Biblical Roots of the Mass

Drink My Blood: Jesus Unveils a New Way

Because of his Bread of Life discourse, John notes that Jesus was a marked man: "After this Jesus went about in Galilee; he would not go about in Judea because the Jews sought to kill him" (John 7:1). Why would many of the Jews seek to kill Jesus? Because they perceived that he was, in effect, urging them to reject the Mosaic covenant. His command to eat his body and drink his blood would be, they believed, a violation of Old Covenant law that would cut them off from Israel. They had thought that Jesus had come at long last, as prophesied, to restore Israel to Davidic kingdom status (see Amos 9:11–12; Isa. 11:1), a status that had not existed since the sixth century B.C. Consequently Jesus' words about his Body and Blood had not merely disappointed many Jews; they also effectively served as a declaration of war. Jesus had not come to fulfill the law as he had claimed (see Matt. 5:17), many Jews thought, but rather to abolish it and thus Israel as they knew it. A "false prophet" such as this, they thought, was worthy of death (see Deut. 13:1–5).

The misunderstanding of many of the ancient Jews is, in part, understandable. Going back to the time of Noah, God had prohibited the consumption of blood (Gen. 9:4). In Leviticus 17:10–14, this prohibition is reiterated and more fully explained. No Israelite, nor any foreigner who sojourned with Israel, could consume blood, lest life be cut off. Why? For God had taught them, "the life of the flesh is in the blood; and I have given it for you upon the altar to make atonement for your souls; for it is the blood that makes atonement by reason of the life" (Lev. 17:11; see Heb. 9:11–12). God designated animal blood to atone for the Israelites' sins; blood represented the life of the animal, which was given for the sake of man's life.

Offering the blood of sacrificed animals turned one toward God in repentance; consuming that same blood posed problems. To partake of an animal's blood meant to seek the "virtues" of that animal—for example, the strength and courage of a bull. Such consumption would lead one to focus on certain animals in an idolatrous manner, as the ancient Egyptians did in serving their animal gods, which represented demons. In idolatrously seeking one's life from a lower life form instead of God, man would be drawn down to the moral level of that species, to act like a beast, as is observed in the occult world.

When he first expounded on the Eucharist, Jesus was well aware of the long-standing biblical prohibitions regarding the consumption of blood. While many misunderstood him as attempting to abrogate these laws, Jesus was actually seeking to fulfill these laws by calling the Jewish people to a higher level of communion with God. The Mosaic legislation of the Old Covenant was not intended by God to last forever. Indeed, the prophet Jeremiah had foretold a "new covenant" that would fulfill the old one God had made with Israel after liberating them from Egypt (Jer. 31:31–34; see Ezek. 36:24–28). In bidding his apostles to eat his Body and drink his Blood, Jesus signaled that the time had arrived to establish "the new covenant in my blood" (Luke 22:20).

Given the common perception that consuming the Eucharist would cut one off from Israel instead of fulfilling the Old Covenant, Jesus' invitation to his first disciples required great faith, an invitation that challenged them to move beyond their image of a political messiah and embrace him as the true Messiah. No longer would the blood of animals signify life for man; rather, the Blood of Jesus himself, poured out in the New Covenant, would actually *provide* life for man (John 6:51). What the blood of animals signified, the Blood of Christ provides. Because his Blood provides redemption, Jesus commands us to drink it (John 6:51, 54).

In contrast to a mortal sin such as adultery, which is always wrong, there was and is nothing intrinsically wrong with drinking animal blood. The prohibition regarding the consumption of blood is a changeable discipline that God imposed to prepare Israel and the whole world for the New Covenant (see Gal. 3:23–26). (The main offense in drinking animal blood for a Jew was disobeying an Old Covenant precept of God. Similarly, a Catholic who eats meat on Lenten Fridays today disregards the Church's God-given, New Covenant authority to bind and loose on disciplinary matters for the good of the faithful [see Matt. 16:19; 18:15–18].) With the coming of Jesus, the blood of animals no longer had any sacrificial significance, because *eternal life* is in the Blood of the Messiah (see Heb. 9:11–15).

The lifting of Old Covenant disciplines was further revealed to St. Peter in a dream, in which God himself declared "unclean" foods acceptable to eat (Acts 10:9–16; see 10:1–48). What concerned God was not maintaining external ritual purity by observing disciplines that were passing away with the fulfillment of the Old Covenant, such as circumcision and ritual hand washing, but rather, fostering internal purity from sin, which comes from Baptism and living a morally upright life in God's grace (see Matt. 23:13–36). To avoid scandals with new Jewish converts and potential Jewish converts, the early Church maintained for a time the discipline prohibiting consumption of blood (Acts 15:28–29).

Jesus shed his blood and "died for our sins once for all" (1 Pet. 3:18), yet he allows us to continue to partake of his timeless

Passover Sacrifice at Mass. We do not partake of Christ's mortal flesh and blood in a carnal fashion; rather, we partake of his risen and glorified Body and Blood under the sacramental appearances of bread and wine. When the devil tempted Jesus to make bread out of stones after forty days of fasting in the wilderness, Jesus told him, "It is written, 'Man shall not live by bread alone, but by every word that proceeds from the mouth of God'" (Matt. 4:4). But when the bread is actually the Word of God made flesh, the Bread come down from heaven, it is also written that on *this Bread alone* man may live forever.

Questions for Reflection and Discussion

1. (a) What Old Testament events prefigure the abundant blessing of the Eucharistic Bread? (b) Why was it suggested that Elisha's actions in 2 Kings 4:42–44 might be the most remarkable Eucharistic prefiguration?

2. (a) How does Jesus' feeding of the five thousand evoke a similar feeding of a multitude by Moses in the Old Testament? (b) Jesus told the Jews that his Father, not Moses, really provided the manna and that he had come as "the true bread from heaven" (John 6:32) to do the same Father's will. How would Jesus' words have likely impacted his Jewish confreres? Explain, using the scriptural clues discussed in John 6.

3. How might one argue that Jesus foretells the New Covenant Passover in John 6:51?

4. How does the dialogue beginning in John 6:51 support belief in the Real Presence of the Eucharist? Consider Jesus' verb usage and the overall context of the passage, including the Jewish people's responses and Jesus' counter-responses.

5. Some argue that John 6:63 — "It is the spirit that gives life, the flesh is of no avail" — illustrates that Jesus' Eucharistic Flesh could not be life giving. Provide a Catholic counterpoint.

6. How would you respond to a Protestant Christian who said Jesus spoke figuratively in John 6 about eating his body and drinking his blood? Use biblical evidence to show how a figurative interpretation of Christ's words leads to an incoherent rendering of the Bread of Life discourse.

7. (a) Explain why many of the Jewish people would have resisted Christ's invitation to drink his blood. What did consuming blood mean in the Old Covenant, and why did they want to kill Christ as a result? (b) Why did Christ's invitation to drink his Blood fulfill, not abrogate, the Old Covenant?

8. (a) Is the biblical ban on drinking animal blood binding on Christians today? Why can Christians consume animal blood today? (b) What constitutes real impurity according to God?

9. How would you argue that only on the Eucharistic Bread can a person live forever?

11

"Do This in Memory of Me"

Jesus Transforms the Passover

Background Reading
    Exodus 12
    Isaiah 52:1–53:12
    Jeremiah 33:14–18; 31:31–34
    Hebrews 7
    Jeremiah 23:1–6
    Malachi 1:1–13; 3:1–5
    Isaiah 66:18–21
    Luke 22:1–39
    Matthew 26:1–30
    John 6

God had once told the prophet Jeremiah that "the Levitical priests shall never lack a man in my presence ... to make sacrifices for ever" (Jer. 33:18). At first glance, the passage appears to cause serious problems for salvation history in general, and the biblical story of the Mass in particular. The Levitical priests served in the Temple, notably offering the Tamid, Passover, and Day of Atonement sacrifices. In addition, the Letter to the

Hebrews teaches that the Levitical priesthood and law were destined to be fulfilled by the law and priesthood according to the order of Melchizedek: "For when there is a change in the priesthood, there is necessarily a change in the law as well" (Heb. 7:12). Jesus was supposed to serve as a priest forever according to Melchizedek (see Heb. 7:17), but how could he do so if God had called Levitical priests "to make sacrifices for ever"? As a descendant of Judah, Jesus lacked the genealogical pedigree to serve as a Levitical priest in the Temple (see Heb. 8:4). How would the Old Covenant transition to the New if the Levitical priesthood continued?

God's Word recorded in Jeremiah 33 was part of a Messianic prophecy and thus related to a "new" covenant (see Jer. 31:33). Consider the context surrounding Jeremiah's mention of Levitical priests:

> Behold, the days are coming, says the LORD, when I will fulfil the promise I made to the house of Israel and the house of Judah. In those days and at that time I will cause a righteous Branch to spring forth for David; and he shall execute justice and righteousness in the land. In those days Judah will be saved and Jerusalem will dwell securely. And this is the name by which it will be called: "The LORD is our righteousness."
>
> For thus says the LORD: David shall never lack a man to sit on the throne of the house of Israel, and the Levitical priests shall never lack a man in my presence to offer burnt offerings, to burn cereal offerings, and to make sacrifices for ever. (Jer. 33:14–18)

The title "the LORD is our righteousness" probably has immediate reference to King Zedekiah, who served at the time of

Jeremiah. But Jeremiah's words also point forward to a more important royal figure. Zedekiah was a king in the line of David. However, contrary to Jeremiah 33:14–18, Israel lacked a man on David's throne after Zedekiah ruled. The Davidic kingdom eventually fell to Babylon in 587 B.C., so Zedekiah could not be the ultimate fulfillment of this passage. As the passage conveys, God said he would fulfill a promise he made to the house of Israel and the house of Judah. Ultimately, that meant restoring David's throne. David was the king of all Israel and a member of the royal tribe of Judah. Long before David lived, God declared that, one day, "the scepter shall not depart from Judah" (Gen. 49:10). In addition, God told David that his throne would ultimately be established forever (2 Sam. 7:12–13).

Although the Davidic kingdom of Israel fell, God declared that David's house would one day be restored (Amos 9:11–12). God delivered on that promise through his Son, Jesus, a member of the house of Judah who received the throne of his forefather David (Luke 1:32–33). Jesus declared that his "kingdom of heaven" would never fall (Matt. 16:18–19). In addition, after his Resurrection and Ascension, Jesus' closest disciples taught that he had fulfilled the words of the prophet Amos in restoring the Davidic kingdom of Israel (Acts 15:15–18).[94]

---

[94] To read more about how the Catholic Church is the prophesied restoration of the Davidic kingdom of Israel, see Catholics United for the Faith's (CUF) FAITH FACT "Rock Solid: Salvation History of the Church." Also worth reading regarding the Church's biblical basis and history is another CUF FAITH FACT: "That They May All Be One: The Difference the Church Makes." Both are free and available online at http://www.cuf.org, or by calling CUF toll-free at (800) MY-FAITH (693-2484).

Jeremiah prophesied about Israel's much-awaited Messiah on another occasion, again invoking the title "the LORD is our righteousness" and noting specifically that he would be a king:

> Behold, the days are coming, says the LORD, when I will raise up for David a righteous Branch, and he shall reign as king and deal wisely, and shall execute justice and righteousness in the land. In his days Judah will be saved, and Israel will dwell securely. And this is the name by which he will be called: "The Lord is our righteousness." (Jer. 23:5–6)

"The LORD is our righteousness" might have evoked memories of Melchizedek, "king of righteousness," who ruled over Salem, which we learned in an earlier chapter was another name for Zion or Jerusalem. To fulfill promises made to the houses of Israel and Judah, the biblical evidence in Jeremiah and elsewhere suggests that God would use a spiritual heir of Melchizedek, but one who would also have to be a descendant of Judah and an heir to the throne of David.

Jeremiah's words in chapters 23 and 33 imply that Levitical priests' "making sacrifices for ever" would somehow be a part of the restoration of the Davidic kingdom of Israel. In addition, in chapter 31, Jeremiah conveys that the restoration of Israel and Judah would include a "new covenant":

> Behold, the days are coming, says the LORD, when I will make a new covenant with the house of Israel and the house of Judah, not like the covenant which I made with their fathers when I took them by the hand to bring them out of the land of Egypt, my covenant which they broke, though I was their husband, says the LORD. But this is

the covenant which I will make with the house of Israel
after those days says the LORD: I will put my law within
them, and I will write it upon their hearts; and I will be
their God, and they shall be my people. And no longer
shall each man teach his neighbor and each his brother,
saying, "Know the LORD," for they shall all know me, from
the least of them to the greatest, says the LORD; for I will
forgive their iniquity, and I will remember their sin no
more. (Jer 31:31–34).

The daily and annual sacrifices at the Temple conveyed that
Levitical sacrifices were incapable of wiping away human sin
so that God would "remember [Israel's] sin no more" (see Heb.
10:1–5). But if the Levitical priesthood were somehow transformed or fulfilled, perhaps it could continue in a new covenant.
The prophet Malachi implies that such a priestly transformation would occur, prophesying that God would one day "purify
the sons of Levi and refine them like gold and silver, till they
present *right offerings* to the Lord" (Mal. 3:3, emphasis added).[95]
Under the Old Covenant—once the "central sanctuary" in
Jerusalem was built (see Deut. 12:5-7)—the only place that
Levitical priests could lawfully offer sacrifices was in the Temple.
Yet Malachi also prophesied that one day a pure offering would
be offered throughout each day among the nations, that is, the
Gentiles (Mal. 1:1), further signaling that the Levitical regime
centered on the Jerusalem Temple was destined to pass away.
The Old Covenant law would not allow for Gentile priests; it

[95] Some scholars view Isaiah 66:18–21 as also supporting the view
that a transformed, fulfilled Levitical priesthood would include
Gentile priests. See A. Penna, "Isaiah," in Fuller et al., eds., *A
New Catholic Commentary on Holy Scripture*, 66, no. 4861.

promised death for priestly interlopers (Num. 3:10; 18:7). Only a new covenant could accommodate Gentiles as transformed Levitical priests offering a new sacrifice.

As the proclaimed "Lamb of God, who takes away the sin of the world" (John 1:29), Jesus provided hope that he might finally bring about this new covenant, in which God would truly forgive Israel's iniquities and thus remember their sins no more. After he revealed that he would restore Israel by establishing his Kingdom of heaven, Jesus began to tell his disciples how he would liberate the world from the spiritual bondage of sin:

> From that time Jesus began to show his disciples that he must go to Jerusalem and suffer many things from the elders and chief priests and scribes, and be killed, and on the third day be raised. (Matt. 16:21)

Long before his Crucifixion, Jesus indicated that he was the suffering servant who "took our infirmities and bore our diseases" (Matt. 8:17; see Isa. 53:4), becoming more explicit as his ministry progressed (Matt. 17:9–13). Before his final trip to Jerusalem, Jesus made clear that he was the suffering-servant lamb, for he "came not to be served but to serve, and to give his life as a ransom for many" (Matt. 20:28; see Isa. 53:12).

Welcoming the Messiah: Jesus Arrives in Jerusalem

Having announced his imminent suffering, Jesus came to Jerusalem to celebrate the Passover one last time, linking his proximate Passion with the annual sacrificial meal: "I have earnestly desired to eat this Passover with you before I suffer" (Luke 22:15; see Luke 12:49–50).

A few days before the Last Supper, the Jewish crowds in Jerusalem could not fathom a kingdom restored through suffering.

They sensed a messiah ("anointed one") in Jesus, but anticipated a political deliverance from Roman oppression. Jesus' powerful preaching and miraculous works had earned the people's devotion, and the Nazarene also had the appropriate messianic pedigree, hailing from the house of David. As the Gospel of Luke would later testify, an angel had proclaimed Jesus the Messianic Savior at his birth (Luke 2:11), and another angel, Gabriel, had previously announced to his Mother that God would give Jesus "the throne of his father David,... and of his kingdom there [would] be no end" (Luke 1:32–33; see 2 Sam. 7:8–16; Matt. 1:1).

As the Jews flocked to Jerusalem for the great feast, they remembered their tradition in great expectation, for the Messiah was to restore Israel's reign on Passover night. Making reference to Jewish Targums, prominent Lutheran scholar Joachim Jeremias explains the fervent anticipation that accompanied the celebration of Passover:

> The Passover at the time of Jesus looked both backwards and forwards. God's people remember at the feast the merciful immunity afforded the houses sprinkled with the blood of the paschal lambs and their deliverance from servitude in Egypt. But that is only one side. At the same time the Passover is a looking forward to the coming deliverance of which the deliverance out of Egypt is the type. This typology is a concept that "most comprehensively determined already in early times, as no other concept did, the form that the doctrine of final salvation took." The Messiah comes on this night! "*On this night they were saved, and on this night they will be saved,*" is an old saying. "The Messiah who is called First (Is. 41:27) will come in the first month (Nisan)." ... Then will the

night turn to day, because the true light shines. Thus the night of the Passover is even called "the sign" by which God guarantees the coming of the Messiah.[96]

As Jeremias, Catholic scholars, and other theologians would all agree, the crucial biblical passage for Messianic anticipation is Exodus 12:42, which discusses the original Passover's provisions: "It was a night of watching by the LORD, to bring them out of the land of Egypt; *so this same night is a night of watching kept to the LORD by all the people of Israel throughout their generations*" (emphasis added).

Given this historical backdrop, one can better understand the jubilant welcome Jesus received at Passover time. When he entered Jerusalem astride a donkey (Matt. 21:1–11; see Zech. 9:9), the Jews excitedly remembered a similar royal ride that inaugurated the reign of another son of David: Solomon (1 Kings 1:38–40); "Hosanna to the Son of David!" they shouted to Jesus (Matt. 21:9). In addition, echoing the words of Psalm 118:26 that were prayed every Passover night, they proclaimed, "Blessed is he who comes in the name of the Lord!" (Matt. 21:9), for they sensed the royal restoration of Israel was finally at hand. It seemed that God's Messiah, that is, the "anointed one," had *finally* arrived.

On that first Palm Sunday, Jesus was considered the long-awaited political liberator, God's "anointed" who would "set at liberty those who are oppressed" (see Luke 4:16–21 and Isa. 61:1–2, 8–9). By week's end, though, the crowds would turn bitterly against Jesus, viewing him as a great failure. Jesus had

---

[96] Jeremias, *The Eucharistic Words of Jesus*, 137–138, emphasis added, footnotes omitted.

not vanquished their Roman oppressors; rather, he was about to die at their hands.

Anticipating Calvary:
Jesus Transforms the Passover

The apostles had heard Jesus speak of his redemptive suffering on various occasions, and on a previous Passover he had shocked many of his disciples by saying that his flesh would actually become bread for the world, providing eternal life (see John 6:51–66). At this Passover, Jesus dramatically transformed, yet continued, the perpetual Passover ordinance first prescribed in Exodus 12. That evening, with Calvary drawing near, Jesus used language that hearkened back to his Bread of Life discourse. As usual, the Passover lamb would be not only sacrificed but eaten; however, given the presence of the new Lamb, *the* Lamb of God, Israel's relationship with God was about to be radically changed:

> And he took bread, and when he had given thanks he broke it, gave it to them, saying, "This is my body which is given for you. Do this in remembrance of me." And likewise the cup after supper, saying, "This cup which is poured out[97] for you is the new covenant in my blood." (Luke 22:19–20; see Exod. 12:5–10)

> Now as they were eating, Jesus took bread, and blessed and broke it, and gave it to the disciples and said, "Take,

---

[97] Christ's "pouring out" parallels the actions of Old Covenant priests, who "poured out" the blood of animal offerings in the wilderness tabernacle and later the Temple (Lev. 4:16–20; Deut. 12:26, 27). As God's definitive sacrificial Lamb, Jesus pours out his blood for all mankind (see Isa. 53:12; 1 Tim. 2:4).

eat; this is my body." And he took a cup, and when he had given thanks he gave it to them, saying, "Drink of it, all of you; for this is my blood of the covenant, which is poured out for many[98] for the forgiveness of sins." (Matt. 26:26–28)

The apostles remembered that, centuries before, their forefather Moses had also shed blood in establishing another covenant. After facilitating Israel's Exodus by sacrificing the Passover lambs (Exod. 12), Moses received the Old Law on Mount Sinai (Exod. 20–23), consummating the covenant with offerings of oxen. To seal Israel's Old Covenant with God, Moses threw "the blood of the covenant" on the people (Exod. 24:8). In establishing Israel's New Covenant, Jesus called his disciples to a profoundly deeper relationship. The ancient ritual of covering the people

---

[98] In some recent English translations of the Eucharistic Prayer, the Latin words *pro multis* — "for many" — were translated as "for all." While various Catholics have criticized this translation, it should be pointed out that the words "for all" do not pose, contrary to what some have argued, a *doctrinal* problem, provided that the words are properly understood. Scripture makes clear that Jesus undoubtedly "desires all men to be saved" (1 Tim. 2:4; see 2 Pet. 3:9; John 3:16). Thus, Jesus certainly "poured out" his blood for all mankind, yet his Sacrifice will be salvifically fruitful "for many." How many is "many"? Jesus died so that sins "may be forgiven." The answer will be determined by how each and every man responds to God's gracious gift of salvation. The bottom line is that the Church teaches both in Scripture and elsewhere that God offers the gift of eternal salvation to all (see CCC 851, 1058, 1256, 1261). To read more on this subject, see CUF's FAITH FACTS *"Pro Multis:* For 'Many' or for 'All'" and "Without the Church There Is No Salvation." These are free and available online at www.cuf.org or by calling CUF toll-free at (800) MY-FAITH (693-2484).

with animal blood would be fulfilled by a much more intimate communion: drinking his Eucharistic Blood. Such consumption would both symbolize and help bring about the internal purification of Israel in the "new covenant," in which God would "remember their sin no more" as Jeremiah had prophesied (Jer. 31:31–34).

While they might have struggled with some of Jesus' words, the apostles may very well have not been surprised that a new covenant would be associated with Passover. Recall that "the Passover is a looking forward to the coming deliverance of which the deliverance out of Egypt is the type."[99] Their ancestors were saved from slavery on Passover, and the Messiah was expected to bring about "final salvation" for Israel on this same night.

In addition, the prophet Isaiah had foretold a new Exodus that harmonized with Jeremiah's prophesied new covenant. The new Exodus would not involve a hasty flight from a mere earthly oppressor (Isa. 52:4; see Exod. 12:11), and its sacrifice would not be a mere lamb or lambs. The new Exodus, a worldwide liberation from sin (Isa. 52:10), would be consummated by the self-offering of a suffering-servant lamb of God (Isa. 53:7). Many in Israel viewed the suffering lamb as symbolic of the suffering their nation had collectively endured since the Davidic kingdom of Judah had fallen in 587 B.C. Yet, as a nation of mere men, Israel had not and could not atone for its own sins, let alone the world's. Neither could their animal sacrifices provide adequate atonement; the repeated offering of their sacrifices served as a reminder of their ineffectiveness. The sacrificial inadequacy of the Day of Atonement offerings particularly stands out:

[99] Jeremias, *Eucharistic Words of Jesus*, 137.

For since the [Old] law has but a shadow of the good things to come instead of the true form of these realities, it can never, by the same sacrifices which are continually offered year after year, make perfect those who draw near. Otherwise, would they not have ceased to be offered? If the worshipers had once been cleansed, they would no longer have any consciousness of sin. But in these sacrifices there is a reminder of sin year after year. For it is impossible that the blood of bulls and goats should take away sins. (Heb. 10:1–4)

The suffering-servant lamb would have to be a very special individual, one who could enter "heaven itself" (Heb. 9:24), entering "once for all into the Holy Place, taking not the blood of goats and calves but his own blood, thus securing an eternal redemption" (Heb. 9:12). Jesus made clear on that Passover evening some two thousand years ago that he was the God-man who would bear the sins of the world (see Isa. 53:7–12).

This Is My Body, This Is My Blood

The Old Covenant Passover celebration was a type of the Eucharistic liturgy: The Day of Atonement was likewise a type of the Eucharist, "a shadow of the good things to come instead of the true form of these realities." At the Last Supper, Passover and the Day of Atonement merge into one, for Christ presents himself as the Lamb of God, who would sacrifice himself (Passover) for the sins of the world (Day of Atonement), and who would be eaten by his disciples (Passover).

Simply *speaking* about eating his Body and drinking his Blood had cost Jesus a great number of followers in the past: "Many of his disciples, when they heard it, said, 'This is a hard saying;

who can listen to it?'... After this many of his disciples drew back and no longer went about with him" (John 6:60, 66). At the Bread of Life discourse, his disciples could not reconcile his words with the Old Covenant proscriptions that barred consumption of blood. Jesus offered no corrections, no clarifications, and watched them walk away. Passover had arrived again, and now Jesus was exhorting his twelve apostles to *eat* his Body and *drink* his Blood. But he did not propose it as an abrogation of the Old Covenant but rather as an advent of the New Covenant. Once again, his closest disciples — the Twelve — remained faithful, except, again, for Judas (see John 6:68–70).

Perhaps our Lord's words at the Last Supper reassured them. While John does not record the institution of the Eucharist in his Gospel, Matthew and Mark make a subtle but significant connection between the miracle of feeding more than five thousand with five loaves and two fish and the celebration of the Last Supper. In each case, the authors use the same Greek verb "cluster," noting that Jesus "took," "blessed," "broke," and "gave" the bread to his followers.[100] In miraculously multiplying the

---

[100] The miracle of the feeding of the five thousand is recorded in Matthew 14:13–21; Mark 6:32–44; and Luke 9:11–17. The institution of the Eucharist is recorded in Matthew 26:26–28; Mark 11:22–24; and Luke 22:19–20. Whereas Luke uses "bless" in his miraculous feeding account like Matthew and Mark, he uses the Greek verb that translates "given thanks" in his account of the Last Supper. Here he parallels St. Paul's account of the Eucharistic institution (1 Cor. 11:24). However, "blessing" and "giving thanks" are two closely related, if not equivalent, ideas in a Jewish context. In addition, our name for the sacrament of Christ's Body and Blood—"Eucharist," which is Greek for "thanksgiving"— derives from the verb Luke and Paul use.

loaves, Jesus provided abundant earthly bread (see John 6:5). Would he provide similarly at the Last Supper? Would the new Exodus and the new Passover have a new meal to celebrate?

The apostles apparently had faith that Jesus not only *could* provide, but that he somehow *would* provide. The day after the miracle of the loaves and fish, Jesus said that he would feed many with his flesh, for he is the living bread come down from heaven (John 6:51). By the time Jesus told them to eat his Body and drink his Blood, perhaps they were ready. They had already seen how Jesus, the proclaimed "Lamb of God," had apparently taken the place of the traditional Passover lamb at the meal, so eating him might have seemed logical, even if a bit mysterious. In any event, we can safely say the apostles knew that something *new* was going on that night — Jesus spoke of "the new covenant in my blood" (Luke 22:20) — and that it was centered on the communion sacrifice of the Passover feast.

The traditional Passover lamb is conspicuous by its absence in any of the Last Supper accounts. While we cannot assume that Christ and his disciples did not first eat a traditional lamb that night, the Gospel writers convey that another Lamb would have the liturgical spotlight in the New Covenant Passover. Because Jesus would be this suffering-servant lamb, offering *his own* Body and Blood would make sense.

"This is my body," Jesus said, raising the bread (see Matt. 26:26 and parallels). "This is my blood," he added, holding up a cup of wine (see Matt. 26:27–28 and parallels). To preserve the sense of Jesus' Aramaic words, Matthew, Mark, and Luke use the Greek words *Tout estin* ("This is"). "The verb *estin*," Catholic apologist Karl Keating notes, "is the Greek equivalent of the English verb 'is' and can mean 'really is' or 'is figuratively'. The usual meaning of *estin* is the former, just as, in English, the verb is usually taken in the real or literal sense." Keating illustrates that, had Jesus wanted to convey unmistakably a figurative meaning, he would not have chosen a verb that is normally used to convey a literal meaning. As Keating adds, "Aramaic has about three dozen words that can mean 'represents', so Christ would have had no difficulty at all in giving an unmistakable equivalent of 'this represents my body'."[101]

The early Church's opponents testified that Christians took Jesus literally regarding the Eucharist. Roman pagans called early Church Christians "cannibals" precisely because the disciples spoke of *eating* and *drinking* their God. In doing so, the pagans provide further evidence that belief in the Real Presence of the Eucharist is an ancient Christian doctrine and that the first Christians understood Jesus to be speaking *literally* when he established at the Last Supper the ritual we have come to call the Mass. Noting the attacks of the Roman historian Tacitus (c. 55–c. 117) and others, Fr. Peter Stravinskas concludes,

> Both Tertullian and Minucius[102] … give considerable attention in their second-century writings to the charge of cannibalism being leveled against the Church. A belief in the Real Presence thus clearly existed in the Early Church, for no "simple memorial supper" would have evoked such specific and violent charges from the general pagan populace.[103]

---

[101] Karl Keating, *Catholicism and Fundamentalism: The Attack on "Romanism" by "Bible Christians"* (San Francisco: Ignatius Press, 1988), 247.

[102] Tertullian and Minucius Felix were early Christian writers.

[103] Fr. Peter Stravinskas, *The Catholic Response* (Huntington, IN: Our Sunday Visitor, 1985), 91.

At the same time, the charge of cannibalism is misapplied to the Eucharist. Cannibals consume the flesh of a *dead* person in a way that diminishes and profanes the corpse. With the Sacrament of the Eucharist, Jesus freely gives himself to us; and we consume his *living,* glorified Body and Blood in a way that mysteriously and miraculously does not diminish him. (For a more in-depth treatment of this aspect of the Eucharistic Mystery, please refer to the following chapter.)

His Passion Draws Near

Jesus also maintained and advanced the Passover in other ways. Wine was not recorded in the first Passover of Exodus 12, yet Israel, not constrained to a "Bible only" view in living out God's commands, developed the ritual over time to include four cups of wine. Prior to Christ's coming, the Book of Jubilees — a nonbiblical yet revered book among the pre-Christian Jewish people — reports that drinking wine at Passover was already an ancient custom (Jub. 49:6, 9).

Along with the use of wine, there developed Passover hymns, specifically the singing of Psalms 113–118 in two parts of what was called the *Hallel*.[104] The people drank four cups, the third of which was the "cup of blessing," which St. Paul identified with the cup that Jesus proclaimed actually contained his Blood of the New Covenant (1 Cor. 10:16; Luke 22:20). Jesus thereby established an inseparable connection between his Sacrifice of Calvary and its prepresentation/anticipation at the Last Supper (see CCC 1337–1340).

---

[104] See Jeremias, *Eucharistic Words of Jesus,* 30–31 (including footnote 1) and 172–175.

The traditional lamb was gone, but the Lamb of God's Self-Sacrifice would allow God to "pass over" and spare the people's lives in a more lasting way, one ordered toward eternal salvation. In identifying the bread and wine with his Body and Blood, Jesus revealed that a single Self-Sacrifice would suffice in liberating Israel and the world from their sins. There would be no need to sacrifice any other lamb, for Jesus had clearly stated that he was inaugurating "the new covenant in my *blood*" (Luke 22:20, emphasis added). At the same time, Jesus indicated that his one Sacrifice could be re-presented again. God had prescribed that the Passover would be "an ordinance for ever," and now Jesus was telling his apostles to "remember" this sacred feast in the new manner he established that night.

A New Lamb to Remember

Here again we see the convergence of the Passover and Day of Atonement sacrificial themes with our Lord's Self-Offering. On the one hand, Jesus is the Lamb of God, who is offered definitively for the atonement of sins. Indeed, at the same Last Supper, Jesus tells his gathered apostles that he is Isaiah's prophesied suffering servant, who "makes himself an offering for sin" (Isa. 53:10): "For I tell you that this scripture must be fulfilled in me, 'And he was reckoned with transgressors'; for what is written about me has its fulfilment" (Luke 22:37; see John 1:29). Recall also that the ancient Jews believed that worldwide redemption would take place one day on Passover night (see Exod. 12:42).[105]

---

[105] Targum Neofiti to Exodus 12:42, as cited in *The Aramaic Bible, Vol. 2 — Targum Neofiti 1: Exodus*, translated with introduction and apparatus by Martin McNamara, M.S.C., and notes by Robert Hayward; Tarpon, *Pseudo-Jonathan: Exodus*,

On the other hand, as the New Passover Lamb, Jesus would not simply be offered; he would also be eaten. And in fulfilling the Passover sacrifice, Jesus' one Offering would be remembered regularly. Jeremias reminds us of God's primacy in liturgical remembrance:

> God's remembrance, however, has always a quite definite meaning in Holy Scripture: it never means a mere recollection on the part of God; but when God remembers somebody, He acts, *He* does something, He sits in judgment and grants His grace, He fulfills His promise. In what way, therefore, is God expected to "remember," when the Messianic community meets and prays to Him that He should "remember His Messiah"? The only possible answer is: God remembers the Messiah by bringing about His kingdom in the parousia.[106] ... That means the Eucharist proclaims the beginning of the time of salvation and prays for the inception of the consummation.[107]

---

translated with notes by Michael Maher, M.S.C. (Collegeville, Minn.: Liturgical Press, 1994), 52–53, emphasis added.

[106] *Parousia* typically refers to Jesus' definitive Second Coming, but it can also refer to a sacramental coming of Jesus in the liturgy.

[107] Jeremias, *Eucharistic Words of Jesus*, 163–164. Jeremias adds, "In the eucharistic prayers of the *Didache* [a document that purports to provide the teaching of the twelve apostles and was written in the first or second century] God is expressly asked for His remembrance (10, 5). The celebrating congregation prays God to remember His Church by granting her fulfillment and by gathering her into His kingdom which He has prepared for her. Here it is unambiguously God who is asked for His remembrance. If we understand the command to repeat the rite like that, it makes sense only if Jesus Himself

"Do This in Memory of Me"

The Lutheran scholar Jeremias did not completely share the Church's belief in the Real Presence, nor did he affirm the Eucharist's sacrificial nature. Yet, he did have a grasp of the profundity that remembrance has in the New Covenant. In every offering of the Eucharistic Sacrifice, the Church proclaims that we experience a sacramental *parousia*, that is, a veiled, sacramental coming of Jesus, in which our Lord continues to carry out the work of our redemption (see CCC 1364). These sacramental comings anticipate and prepare for his ultimate Parousia, his Second Coming (see Heb. 9:28), when he will return unveiled in glory for the Last Judgment and the culmination of his Kingdom as it is lived on earth: "The Kingdom of God has been coming since the Last Supper and, in the Eucharist, it is in our midst. The kingdom will come in glory when Christ hands it over to his Father [at his Second Coming]" (CCC 2816; see 2821, 1038–1050).

Yet, before the Kingdom could culminate at the Last Judgment, it had to come first on earth. From our vantage point today, Jesus' actions at the Last Supper indicated that he would both die and rise triumphantly. How could Jesus' disciples continue to partake of his Body and Blood if his body remained buried? Still, because his Offering was a prepresentation and anticipation, the Last Supper in the Upper Room also indicated that Jesus' work was not complete. The Messiah came in glory on Passover night to establish the Mass. Now he had to "finish" what he had

---

gave it. He desired that His disciples should continue to meet together daily as the table fellowship of the Messiah during the short interval between His departure and the *parousia*, and thereby beseech God to remember His Messiah by bringing the consummation to pass" (164–165).

started in the Upper Room. Now he had to live out the definitive presentation of his one Sacrifice of Calvary.

Questions for Reflection and Discussion

1. God told Jeremiah that he would always provide Levitical priests to make sacrifices, yet the Letter to the Hebrews teaches that there has been a "change" in the priesthood. Can the two biblical passages be reconciled? Explain, incorporating Scripture into your answer. (Hint: Can a priesthood carry on in a fulfilled manner under another name?)

2. Why did Jesus' arrival in Jerusalem on a donkey at Passover time raise Messianic expectations?

3. (a) Why might the Jewish people have expected a new covenant to be inaugurated on Passover? (b) In light of the "new covenant" prophesied by Jeremiah and the offering of the suffering-servant lamb, how do Christ's actions at the Last Supper Passover fulfill salvation history?

4. (a) How do Christ's actions at the Last Supper parallel his miracle of the multiplication of loaves in John 6? What are the implications of this parallel? (b) How do Jesus' words in the Upper Room hearken back to the Bread of Life discourse in John 6?

5. How does the ancient charge of cannibalism support the Church's teaching about the Mass?

6. What role did wine traditionally play in the Passover, and how did Jesus maintain, yet transform, its use?

7. (a) How do the Passover and Day of Atonement sacrifices merge in fulfillment in Christ's Sacrifice of Calvary and

its sacramental re-presentation in the Mass? (b) Explain how Christ's Kingdom comes at every Mass through our "remembering" him, even though Christ will definitively come in glory at the *Parousia*, that is, the Second Coming. (c) In what sense did Jesus have to "finish" on Good Friday (see John 19:30) what he began at the Last Supper?

12

"Source of Eternal Salvation"

Jesus as a Priest Forever
according to the Order of Melchizedek

Background Reading
    John 11:45–53
    Isaiah 52–53
    Matthew 26
    Luke 22
    Hebrews 2:10–15
    Hebrews 5:1–10
    Genesis 14:14–18
    Hebrews 7–8
    Hebrews 10:1–14
    John 6

To preserve their own power in ruling Israel, the Pharisees and the priests joined forces to destroy Jesus (Matt. 12:14; see John 18:14). Ironically, the Crucifixion they engineered hastened their own ministerial demise, for through his sacrificial death Jesus would restore the kingdom of Israel with a new priesthood and teaching authority. The focus of that priesthood would be the

Sacrifice of the Mass, with the apostles ordained as Christ's first priests of the New Covenant, acting in his person and power (CCC 610–611, 1548; see 1566).

That Israel's leaders did not realize that their actions would help usher in a new priesthood and a New Covenant is understandable. Jesus' death considered on its own, let alone as an offering to be done in remembrance of him, did not appear to be a wondrous, redemptive sacrifice:

> From the point of view of the Old Testament cult, the death of Jesus in no way appeared as a sacrifice; it was in fact the very opposite of sacrifice. Indeed, sacrifice did not consist in the putting to death of a living person, still less in his sufferings, but in rites performed by the priest in the holy place.... The rites that accompanied a sacrifice made it a solemn and glorious act, which would bring about a union with God and obtain divine blessings.... Now Jesus' death had taken place outside the Holy City. It had not been accompanied by liturgical rites. It was viewed as a legal penalty, the execution of a man condemned to death.... Far from uniting to God and drawing down his blessings, it was truly a curse. It would seem to follow then that the Calvary event would only increase the distance between Jesus and the priesthood.[108]

The Gospels help make sense of Christ's death. After Jesus raised Lazarus from the dead and his popularity grew, the high

---

[108] Albert Vanhoye, *Old Testament Priests and the New Priest: According to the New Testament,* trans. J. Bernard Orchard, O.S.B. (Petersham, MA: St. Bede's Publications, 1986), 50–51.

priest Caiaphas unknowingly prophesied the sacrificial nature of Christ's death:

> Many of the Jews therefore, who had come with Mary and had seen what he did [raising Lazarus], believed in him; but some of them went to the Pharisees and told them what Jesus had done. So the chief priests and the Pharisees gathered the council, and said, "What are we to do? For this man performs many signs. If we let him go on thus, everyone will believe in him, and the Romans will come and destroy both our holy place [the Temple] and our nation." But one of them, Caiaphas, who was high priest that year, said to them, "You know nothing at all; you do not understand that it is expedient for you that one man should die for the people, and that the whole nation should not perish." He did not say this of his own accord, but being high priest that year he prophesied that Jesus should die for the nation, and not for the nation only, but to gather into one the children of God who are scattered abroad. So from that day on they took counsel how to put him to death. (John 11:45–53)

Jesus would die not only for the people of Israel but for the whole world (see John 3:16). At the Last Supper, gathered with his apostles, Jesus said that his Blood would be "poured out for many for the forgiveness of sins" (Matt. 26:28). In saying "for many," a number of Scripture scholars believe Jesus is making a subtle reference to the suffering servant, who "makes himself an offering for sin" and "bore the sin of many" (Isa. 53:10, 12).[109]

---

[109] Ibid., 54.

The reference becomes less debatable when, quoting Isaiah 53:12, Jesus goes on to identify himself explicitly at the Last Supper as the suffering servant Isaiah prophesied: "For I tell you that this scripture must be fulfilled in me, 'And he was reckoned with transgressors'; for what is written about me has its fulfilment" (Luke 22:37).

In addition, in uniting "blood" with "covenant," Jesus makes an explicit, sacrificial gesture. His words have "an obvious connection with the words pronounced by Moses at the sacrifice accomplished on Sinai as a way of sealing the [Old] covenant between the People of Israel and Yahweh. 'This is,' said Moses, 'the blood of the covenant which the Lord has concluded with you.'"[110] Now Jesus was saying, "This cup which is poured out for you is the new covenant in my blood" (Luke 22:20). Pope John Paul II affirms and elaborates on the sacrificial and covenant implications of Christ's words at the Last Supper:

> A *causal influence of the Eucharist* is present at the Church's very origins. The evangelists specify that it *was* the Twelve, the apostles, who gathered with Jesus at the Last Supper (cf. Matt. 26:20; Mark 14:17; Luke 22:14). This is a detail of notable importance, for the apostles "were both the seeds of the new Israel and the beginning of the sacred hierarchy." By offering them his body and his blood as food, Christ mysteriously involved them in the sacrifice which would be completed later on Calvary. [Here the pope speaks of the earthly phase's completion.] By analogy

---

[110] Vanhoye, *Old Testament Priests*, 53–54. Vanhoye cites the latter part of Exodus 24:8. The RSVCE renders the passage as follows: "Behold the blood of the covenant which the Lord has made with you in accordance with all these words."

with the Covenant of Mount Sinai, sealed by sacrifice and the sprinkling of blood, the actions and words of Jesus at the Last Supper laid the foundations of the new messianic community, the People of the New Covenant.[111]

To redeem the world and enable his apostles to carry on the work of his redemption through offering the Mass, Jesus willingly submitted to the suffering imposed upon him as part of God's plan (CCC 599–600). While the priests and the Pharisees were instrumental in his Crucifixion, the Church adamantly rejects any attempts to make the Jewish people collectively or solely responsible for his death (CCC 597). All men and women who have sinned, including Catholics, share responsibility for Christ's death (see CCC 598, 615).

Priest and Victim

In offering himself willingly for our sins, we can see once again that Jesus' Sacrifice did not begin and end on the Cross. As a divine Person, Jesus needed no perfecting. But the human nature he assumed in becoming man was still mortal and thus susceptible to suffering. He offered his body for our salvation on the Cross and made it "perfect through suffering" (Heb. 2:10; see 5:8–10; 10:10). His bodily perfection came at his Resurrection,[112] when he rose in glory, illustrating in another way that his Sacrifice was not completed on Calvary. Jesus had to be perfected before he could present his completed Self-Offering to the Father

---

[111] Pope John Paul II, encyclical letter *Ecclesia de Eucharistia* (Boston: Pauline Books and Media, 2003), no. 21, emphasis in original, footnotes omitted.

[112] See Fr. James Swetnam, S.J., "Christology and the Eucharist in the Epistle to the Hebrews," *Biblica* 70, no. 1 (1980): 74–95.

in the heavenly sanctuary. To paraphrase St. Paul: if no Resurrection, then no perfection of Christ or us, his disciples: "If Christ has not been raised, then our preaching is in vain and your faith is in vain.... But in fact Christ has been raised from the dead, the first fruits of those who have fallen asleep" (1 Cor. 15:20).

The perfection could become ours once Jesus completed his Offering in the heavenly sanctuary. Recall that the Day of Atonement sacrifices were not considered completed until the blood of the slaughtered victims had been sprinkled upon and in front of God's mercy seat in the holy of holies. Similarly, even after his Resurrection and having attained a glorified body, Jesus tells Mary Magdalene that his work is not yet complete: "Jesus said to her, 'Do not hold me, for I have not yet ascended to the Father; but go to my brethren and say to them, I am ascending to my Father and your Father, to my God and your God'" (John 20:17; see CCC 659–664). Remember also that Pentecost and the empowerment of God's Kingdom occurred only *after* Christ's Ascension (CCC 1076).

The Letter to the Hebrews teaches that Jesus' Ascension was necessary to complete God's saving plan, which included our Lord's perfecting the Day of Atonement sacrifices by entering a sanctuary not made with human hands, that is, a heavenly sanctuary, to atone for the world's sins (Heb. 9:11–12, 23–24; see also 10:12). The letter also elaborates on the inadequacy of the Old Covenant offerings, referring to both the daily Tamid lamb sacrifices and the annual Day of Atonement offerings. Israel's need to slaughter and offer new animals every day (see Heb. 7:27) and every year (see Heb. 9:25), the author of Hebrews teaches, illustrates the sacrificial ineffectiveness of these sin offerings and points toward their heavenly perfection by Christ in the New Covenant:

[The priests of the Temple] serve [in] a copy and shadow of the heavenly sanctuary; for when Moses was about to erect the tent, he was instructed by God, saying, "See that you make everything according to the pattern which was shown you on the mountain" [Exod. 25:40]. But as it is, Christ has obtained a ministry which is as much more excellent than the old as the covenant he mediates is better, since it is enacted on better promises. For if that first covenant had been faultless, there would have been no occasion for a second. (Heb. 8:5–7; see 10:1–5, 11)

Jesus completes his Sacrifice and perfects the Day of Atonement offerings when he, the high priest of the New Covenant, ascends to the ultimate holy of holies, "into heaven itself" (Heb. 9:24), to offer himself to the Father on our behalf: "[H]e entered once for all into the Holy Place,[113] taking not the blood of goats and calves[114] but his own blood, thus securing an eternal redemption" (Heb. 9:12). Jesus' human nature was not perfected in isolation but, reaffirming the priestly nature of his actions, for the benefit of all men and women, for "we have been sanctified through the offering of the *body* of Jesus Christ once for all" (Heb. 10:10, emphasis added). "God renews mankind in Christ in order to introduce him for ever into His presence (Heb. 9:24)," adds one scholar. "The transformation in question consists in a radical renewal of human nature, which makes it fit for perfect communion with God."[115]

---

[113] Here the Letter to the Hebrews uses the term *holy place* as a reference to the "most holy place," as we will see (see Heb. 9:3).

[114] *Calves* is a collective reference to the young bulls offered year after year on the Day of Atonement.

[115] Vanhoye, *Old Testament Priests and the New Priest*, 131. See CCC 412.

Only in ascending to complete his priestly Offering can Jesus take his throne and fully inaugurate his Kingdom (CCC 664, see 1076). Citing our Lord's words recorded in John's Gospel, the *Catechism* provides, "'And I, when I am lifted up from the earth, will draw all men to myself' [John 12:32]. The lifting up of Jesus on the cross signifies and announces his lifting up by his Ascension into heaven, and indeed begins it" (CCC 662). Jesus thus conveys that the Crucifixion, Resurrection, and Ascension are distinct but inseparable aspects of his one, triumphant Sacrifice of Calvary, his Paschal Mystery. The renowned British apologist Frank Sheed elaborates further:

> We tend to think of the Resurrection and the Ascension as simply happy sequels to Calvary. But more and more they have been seen *as the sacrifice's necessary completion.* All sacrifices for sin had meant the offering of a victim to God. Only a couple of times in the Old Testament did God show his acceptance of the sacrifice, by sending fire from heaven (Lev. 9:24, 2 Chron. 7:1). In this, the perfect sacrifice, of which all others were only prefigurings, God showed it by bringing the victim back to life. But with the Ascension God shows himself as accepting not only the sacrifice but the Victim. He took the victim to himself: there was no way of doing that in the earlier sacrifices[116] — what would God have done with a roasted ox or a blood-drained goat?

---

[116] Actually, every Temple sacrifice burned on the altar ascended to God. The burning translated the sacrificial victim into a "pleasing odor" that ascended to God (see Lev. 1:9). Sheed apparently means that with no other sacrifice did God take the *entire victim* to himself.

It was a perfect sacrifice, it was offered for the world's redemption.[117]

Fr. Nicholas Gihr, an eminent twentieth-century liturgist, affirms that the Resurrection and the Ascension are integral parts of Christ's Sacrifice of Calvary:

> The Eucharistic Sacrifice is the living commemoration and mystical accomplishment of the entire work of redemption; Christ as high priest and as victim is present on the altar with all the fruits and merits of the redemption. In the Holy Sacrifice of the Mass, not only His passion and death, but also the life of His glory is mystically represented and renewed. Three great mysteries are here made prominent: before all, the sufferings of Christ in His Sacrifice and death on the cross, as the essence and center of the work of redemption; then the joyful resurrection and glorious ascension, which constitute the conclusion and crown of the work of redemption.[118]

A Heavenly Offering Is a Perpetual Offering

In ascending to the heavenly sanctuary and presenting his perfected Self-Sacrifice to the Father, Jesus completes Calvary; yet, because it culminates in the timeless, never-ending realm of heaven, his Offering necessarily has a perpetual character.

---

[117] Frank J. Sheed, *What Difference Does Jesus Make?* (Huntington, IN.: Our Sunday Visitor, 1974), 196, emphasis added.

[118] Rev. Dr. Nicholas Gihr, *The Holy Sacrifice of the Mass: Dogmatically, Liturgically, and Ascetically Explained*, translated from the German (St. Louis: B. Herder, 1949), 685–686, footnotes omitted.

Through his Ascension, "Christ has entered ... into heaven it-self, *now* to appear in the presence of God on our behalf" (Heb. 9:24, emphasis added). *Now*, because Jesus "always lives to make intercession for [us]" (Heb. 7:25). *Now*, because Jesus "holds his priesthood permanently" (Heb. 7:24; see 8:3). *Now*, because if Jesus only offered a "once for all" Sacrifice as high priest,[119] his Sacrifice *must* have a perpetual character, for how else could he *always* make *priestly* intercession for us in the heavenly sanctuary without a sacrificial offering (see Heb. 8:1–3)? Scripture settles the matter: "It is necessary" for the high priest of heaven "to have something to offer" *now* (Heb. 8:3; see 8:6). As St. Paul affirms elsewhere, Jesus' priestly ministry continues now in the heavenly sanctuary, for he "indeed intercedes for us ... at the right hand of God" (Rom. 8:34; see CCC 1090).

Recall the discussion from chapter 7, which distinguished between the timebound, historical, earthly phase of Christ's Sacrifice (suffering, death, and Resurrection) and the never-ending, heavenly phase of Christ's Sacrifice (activated when he entered the heavenly sanctuary). Christ's disciples witnessed and recorded the historical aspects of his one Sacrifice. But would the heavenly, perpetual phase of his Sacrifice impact the world in any visible way? Could the Sacrifice be celebrated on earth? The Letter to the Hebrews helps answer this question too:

In the days of his flesh, Jesus offered up prayers and sup-plications, with loud cries and tears, to him who was able to save him from death, and he was heard for his godly fear. Although he was a Son, he learned obedience through what he suffered; and being made perfect he

[119] See Heb. 7:27; 9:11, 28; 10:10, 12.

became the source of eternal salvation to all who obey him, being designated by God a high priest after the order of Melchizedek. (Heb. 5:7–10)

This is perhaps the most profound passage in the biblical story of the Mass. In proclaiming that Christ's perfected Sacrifice made him the source of eternal salvation and, thereby, a priest forever according to the order of Melchizedek (Heb. 5:9–10), the Letter to the Hebrews reveals that Calvary and the Last Supper are intimately linked in a truly sublime, sacrificial manner. Christ explicitly linked the Last Supper event with his imminent Sacrifice of Calvary, offering his Body and Blood under the Melchizedekian signs of bread and wine (Luke 22:19–20; see Gen. 14:18). Hebrews tells us that Christ's Melchizedekian priesthood was enacted in light of Calvary and that he will somehow continue his priestly ministry of Calvary — that is, the work of eternal salvation, in a Melchizedekian manner.

Making Heaven a Place on Earth: The Priesthood according to Melchizedek

Through the New Covenant Passover ordinance of the Mass, Jesus enables the Church to make present the never-ending Sacrifice of Calvary. As he was designated a priest forever according to the order of Melchizedek, so Jesus designates men, beginning with his apostles, to act *in persona Christi* ("in the person of Christ") as New Covenant priests (see CCC 1548). The Church's priests celebrate the Mass as the Passover ordinance transformed and fulfilled, making present, offering up, and consuming the timeless Sacrifice of the Lamb of God under the Melchizedekian signs of bread and wine, just as Jesus first did at the Last Supper and designated his apostles to do thereafter. As the *Catechism* (no. 662) provides, "As 'high priest of the good things to come' he is the center and the principal actor of the liturgy that honors the Father in heaven [Heb. 9:11; cf. Rev. 4:6–11]." Jesus not only fulfills his Father's will in heaven, but, living up to the Lord's Prayer, does so "on earth as in heaven" through his priests, beginning with the apostles. (Ultimately, though, earth is fulfilled by being drawn up to heaven. That is, while Scripture describes Jesus as a "priest for ever according to the order of Melchizedek," "for ever"[120] means only until the end of time in one sense, for in heaven the sacramental veils of bread and wine will give way to perfected, face-to-face communion with our beloved Lord [see 1 Cor. 13:12]. Jesus perfects the priesthood of Melchizedek in heaven in another way because in the heavenly sanctuary, "he continues a priest for ever" [Heb. 7:3], that is, for all eternity.)

The Melchizedekian priesthood also reveals how the Passover ordinance would continue in the New Covenant, how time and eternity would intersect in the Mass through the re-presentation of Christ's one, perpetual Sacrifice. Remember the analogy of the sun. As we become present anew to the ongoing reality of the sun every morning, so also we become present anew to the Son's ongoing, heavenly reality of Calvary completed — the Lamb standing as though slain — every time we celebrate Mass.

---

[120] As discussed in chapter 6, "for ever" does not necessarily mean for all eternity when used in the Bible. For example, God decreed that Passover — with its sacrifice and consumption of *animal* lambs — would be an "ordinance for ever" (Exod. 12:14, 17, 24). Yet we see that this particular Passover ordinance ended shortly after Christ, "our paschal lamb" (1 Cor. 5:7), arrived to fulfill it with his one Sacrifice. "For ever" was as long as the sacrificial system of the Old Covenant existed.

Note too that, in describing the Last Supper that Jesus celebrated in a Passover context, the Gospel writers make no mention of a traditional lamb, implying what Paul makes explicit: Christ is the new Passover Lamb (1 Cor. 5:7). Note further that, in transforming the Passover ritual that evening, Christ made no provision to do away with the "ordinance forever" aspect of the sacrificial meal. To the contrary, he explicitly tells his apostles to continue the new celebration as a "remembrance" of his sacrificial death. Note further still that Jesus never stipulates that he is doing away with the Passover provisions of offering and consuming a sacrificial Lamb. To the contrary, Jesus, whom John described as "the Lamb of God, who takes away the sin of the world" (John 1:29), tells his apostles (1) that he is mysteriously offering himself at the Last Supper and bids them to partake of himself under the Melchizedekian signs of bread and wine and (2) that they are to continue this Offering as a traditional Jewish remembrance, not simply as a mere memorial.

The general Protestant rejoinder is that Christ's Sacrifice and associated salvific work were completed with his death and Resurrection.[121] Thus, the Mass cannot be a sacrifice in any sense. For those Christians who do not believe in the Mass, Catholics should charitably ask some questions. The Church teaches that bread and wine are the signature, sacrificial matter of the Melchizedekian priesthood as it is lived out on earth, citing Genesis 14:18 and Christ's use of bread and wine at the Last Supper (CCC 1333, 1350). If bread and wine are not such matter, what

---

[121] While Protestants do not believe that Christ's Sacrifice has an ongoing character, they do believe that the *merits* or *fruits* of Christ's Sacrifice are ongoing and infinite, and that they can tap into them on an ongoing basis, most importantly in accepting Christ as personal Lord and Savior.

are the distinguishing features of a Melchizedekian sacrifice, particularly regarding Christ's once-for-all Sacrifice of Calvary? That is, given what the Letter to the Hebrews provides in 5:8–10, how is Christ's Melchizedekian priesthood associated with his being the source of eternal salvation? In addition, because Jesus holds his priesthood *permanently*, in what way does he *continue* to make intercession for us in a distinctively Melchizedekian manner on earth, if not through the sacramental re-presentation of his one Sacrifice that is ever offered to the Father in heaven? Remember, a priest is primarily appointed to "offer gifts and sacrifices; hence it is necessary for *this priest* to have something to offer" (Heb. 8:3, emphasis added), and he must do so in a Melchizedekian manner.[122] Further, if the continued, *earthly* offering of Jesus' one Sacrifice has no biblical basis, how has the Melchizedekian priesthood fulfilled the Levitical priesthood on earth (see Heb. 7:11–12)? And, if there are no New Covenant priests serving the Father in and with Christ on earth, how did God fulfill Malachi 3:3 and "purify the sons of Levi and refine them like gold and silver, till they present[ed] right offerings to the Lord"? Finally, if not the Mass, what is the "pure offering" that is offered among the nations on earth on an apparently daily basis, that is, "from the rising of the sun to its setting" (Mal. 1:11)?

In contrast, the Catholic celebration of the Mass makes biblical and historical sense of the interdependent themes of (1) the transformed Passover ordinance, in which Jesus prepresented

---

[122] As noted, while Christ's Sacrifice is made present and offered on earth under the appearances of bread and wine until the end of time (that is, offered until Christ's Second Coming), in *heaven* Jesus offers it in perfected Melchizedekian fashion, that is, without the sacramental veils of bread and wine and without end.

and anticipated his Communion Sacrifice at the Last Supper and which the apostles not only consumed in the Upper Room that evening but also continued thereafter according to Christ's command; (2) his *completed* Sacrifice of Calvary, that is, completed in everlasting glory at the Ascension, thereby enabling his work of redemption/atonement to continue both in heaven and on earth; and (3) Christ's service as a priest forever according to the order of Melchizedek, which Scripture reveals is enacted in light of his becoming the source of eternal salvation through the same Sacrifice of Calvary, and which the Church re-presents under the Melchizedekian appearances of bread and wine at every Mass, just as Jesus commanded.

A Once-for-all Offering, yet Offered for Acceptance at Every Mass?

Some Protestant critics persist in their criticism of the Mass, citing what they perceive are doctrinal contradictions in the Church's traditional Eucharistic Prayer—the Roman Canon, which is now known as Eucharistic Prayer I in the Mass rite that Pope Paul VI promulgated. *After* the Consecration, the Church asks our heavenly Father to "look with favor on these offerings and accept them as" he once accepted the offerings of Abel, Abraham, and Melchizedek. This appeal for acceptance contradicts Church teaching, the critics argue, because the Father has already accepted his Son's Sacrifice and the prayer puts the priest in the impossible position of serving as a mediator between Christ and the Father (see 1 Tim. 2:5).[123] There is a second

---

[123] Cf. Rev. Josef A. Jungmann, S.J., *The Mass of the Roman Rite: Its Origins and Development*, replica ed. (Allen, TX Christian Classics, 1986), 227.

alleged contradiction, which immediately follows in Eucharistic Prayer I. The Church prays, "[A]lmighty God, command that these gifts be borne by the hands of your holy Angel to your altar on high." The critics argue that this prayer petition contradicts the Church's teaching that Christ's Sacrifice is ever before the Father in heaven, having culminated in everlasting glory. Rather, the critics add, the prayer implies that the Church repeats the heavenly phase of Christ's Sacrifice at every Mass, with Christ ascending anew with an angel's aid to the heavenly sanctuary.

Let's consider each charge in turn. The Church clearly teaches that the Mass is the selfsame Sacrifice of Christ that culminated in everlasting glory in the heavenly sanctuary (see CCC 1366–1367). Consequently, the Mass does not attempt to provide a distinct reoffering of Christ apart from his one Sacrifice, as if the earthly or the heavenly phase, or both, could be replicated. Rather, at Mass, the Church *participates* in and makes present Christ's one everlasting Sacrifice. That is, that which exists in everlasting glory in heaven becomes miraculously present on an earthly altar under the sacramental appearances of bread and wine. Because it is the *same* Sacrifice, the Church necessarily offers it in union with and by the power of Jesus (see CCC 1548). As the brilliant German theologian Fr. Matthias Scheeben affirms, in the Mass we humbly ask the Father to accept *our* participation in his Son's already existing and everlasting Offering:

> For there is no question of giving Christ anew to His Father as His own, but of exhibiting and ratifying the union of the Church with the gift of Christ *that has already been handed over to God....* By the celebration of the sacrificial act which takes place on this earth, the Church is

to enter directly into union with the heavenly sacrifice Christ offers.[124]

In asking the Father to accept her participation in his Son's everlasting Offering, therefore, the Church, united to Christ, also offers herself to the Father:

The Eucharist is also the sacrifice of the Church. The Church which is the Body of Christ participates in the offering of her Head. With him, she herself is offered whole and entire.... The lives of the faithful, their praise, sufferings, prayer, and work, are united with those of Christ and with his total offering, and so acquire a new value. (CCC 1368, emphasis in original)

Yet a priest and congregation cannot presume upon the Father's acceptance of their participation in his Son's one Offering. We are sinners, so we humbly ask that God accept our sacrificial participation:

Since we are often wanting in the proper dispositions, in piety, purity of heart, fervor of devotion, let us make humble supplications to the Most High, that He be not offended on account of our sinfulness, and reject not the Eucharistic gifts from our unworthy hands, but that He look upon and graciously accept them presented by us, that they may, not only as the sacrifice of Christ but also as our sacrifice, bring down upon us bountiful blessings and a superabundance of grace....[125]

---

[124] Matthias Joseph Scheeben, *The Mysteries of Christianity*, trans. Cyril Voilert (St. Louis, MO: B. Herder, 1946), 509, emphasis added. See also Gihr, *The Holy Sacrifice of the Mass*, 697.

[125] Gihr, *The Holy Sacrifice of the Mass*, 692, footnote omitted.

Such petitions ... are perfectly justifiable, inasmuch as we offer the Eucharistic sacrifice and ourselves in union with it. To do this worthily, we should possess perfect sanctity, but as this is wanting to us, we recommend our sacrifice to the favor and indulgence of God, that it may be more agreeable to Him and more salutary to us.[126]

The plea for the Father's acceptance presumes that a valid Consecration has taken place at a Mass. Yet, as noted, one cannot presume that the Father will accept the sacrificial participation in his Son's one Offering of a particular priest and his congregation.[127] In summary, the petition for the Father's acceptance

---

[126] Gihr, *The Holy Sacrifice of the Mass*, 693.

[127] For example, one cannot presume that God will accept the sacrificial participation of a priest who has recently and formally gone into schism. The offering and partaking of the Eucharist signifies and brings about unity with Christ (see CCC 1396, 1398), yet a Mass offered by such a schismatic priest, when done with full knowledge of the wrongdoing and with complete consent of the will, is a grave offense against unity (see CCC 1854–1861), for it is deliberately offered against the express directive of the Pope (see Matt. 10:19), the earthly leader of Christ's Church, and thus not in full communion with Christ and his Church. While such a schismatic priest may attempt to offer the Mass reverently, his disobedient liturgical action is, focusing specifically on his subjective participation, a sacrilege (see CCC 2120). Thus, Christ's Sacrifice is always acceptable to the Father when considered in itself, even when sacramentally re-presented by such a schismatic priest. As the Council of Trent teaches, "This is indeed that clean oblation which cannot be defiled by any unworthiness or malice on the part of those who offer it" ("Doctrine Concerning the Sacrifice of the Mass," chap. 1, as cited in *The Canons and Decrees of the Council of Trent*, trans. Rev. H. J. Schroeder, O.P. [Rockford, IL: TAN Books and Publishers, 1978], 145; see CCC 1128). But a

is no idle plea. The petition is not on behalf of Christ's Offering, which has already been accepted. The plea is for accepting

---

schismatic priest should not presume that God will affirm *his personal participation in* that Offering. Such a priest is to be distinguished from those priests in the separated Eastern churches who bear no personal responsibility for initiating a schism (see CCC 814). Yet, as with recently and formally schismatic priests, the Catholic Church greatly desires full communion with such Eastern priests (see CCC 846–848, 1398–1399).

Recent and formally schismatic priests may counter that dissenting priests who irreverently offer the Mass while "in communion with the Pope" could also be found wanting by our heavenly Father. While an argument can be made in that regard, the Father would presumably make distinctions in such cases between the personal participation of the offending priest and that of the lay faithful who obediently and reverently participate in a Mass that is offered in communion with the Pope, that is, offered by a priest who is in juridical communion with his bishop and who in turn is recognized as being in communion with the Pope by the Pope himself.

The issue is admittedly a complicated one, for priests who persevere in schism are presumably more culpable than many of their parishioners, whose love for the Tridentine liturgy and whose grief over liturgically abusive activity at their respective parishes in communion with the Pope may have contributed to their aligning themselves with a schismatic parish. Even though these lay faithful may have mitigating circumstances regarding their participation in schismatic liturgies, their support of schismatic activities can neither be condoned nor encouraged (see CCC 817, 2089). In addition, while priests and parishioners partake of a valid Eucharist in such schismatic liturgies, their willful, ongoing, and sinful support of schismatic activity will impair to varying degrees their benefiting from that sacrament, irrespective of whether they have been formally excommunicated. The same generally applies to any Catholic at any Mass who receives the Eucharist without having repented of any sin.

our participation in that one Offering, which cannot be taken for granted, similar to the way Old Covenant priests could not presume that their offerings would be automatically accepted by the Father.

The response to the second charge of doctrinal contradiction is implicit in the response to the first charge. The Mass is not a distinct reoffering of the heavenly phase of Christ's Sacrifice, as if Jesus ascends heavenward on the wings of an angel every time the Mass is celebrated. Rather, as noted above, the Mass is the Church's participation in Christ's one Sacrifice that culminated in everlasting glory in the heavenly sanctuary at his one and only Ascension. So what role does the angel play? The plea for angelic assistance recalls the celestial vision of St. John in the book of Revelation in which he describes how angels bring forth the prayers of the saints on earth to the heavenly altar (Rev. 8:3–5). Following on the provision of Revelation 8:3–5 and using figurative language, the Church invokes angelic assistance in having the Father find acceptable our participation in his Son's Sacrifice.

Fr. Josef Jungmann, S.J., affirms that the plea for God's angel to take the Sacrifice to the heavenly sanctuary is "a figurative way of expressing God's acceptance ('*Supplices*')" of the Church's participation in Christ's everlasting Sacrifice.[128] Fr. Jungmann adds elsewhere, "A gift is fully accepted not when it has drawn itself a friendly glance, but when it is actually taken into the recipient's possession."[129] An angel does not physically take the Eucharist to heaven, for there is a mystical unity between

---

[128] Josef Jungmann, S.J., *The Mass: An Historical, Theological, and Pastoral Survey*, trans. Rev. Julian Fernandes, S.J., ed. Mary Ellen Evans (Collegeville, MN: Liturgical Press, 1976), 196.

[129] Jungmann, *The Mass of the Roman Rite*, 231.

Christ's everlasting Offering in the heavenly sanctuary and its sacramental re-presentation on altars throughout the world. Rather, the angel mystically intercedes for us at Mass as angels do for us in Revelation 8. With the aid of angelic assistance, the Church's participation in Christ's one Sacrifice — and the Church herself — are taken into the possession of the Father.

Theologians debate the identity of "the angel."[130] Most importantly, though, the Mass is not possible without Christ and the power of the Holy Spirit (see CCC 1353). And, in addition to the interceding angel, many angels participate in the celebration of the Mass (see Rev. 5:11–14). Indeed, as both Pope St. Gregory the Great and St. John Chrysostom eloquently attest, an angelic host is always present when heaven and earth unite in the offering of Christ's one Sacrifice at Mass:

> What believing soul can doubt that at the hour of the Sacrifice, upon the word of the priest, heavens open and that choirs of angels assist at this mystery of Jesus Christ, that here the highest is combined with the lowest, the earthly united with the heavenly, the visible and the invisible become one?[131]

> The priest is himself at that solemn moment surrounded by angels, and the choir of the heavenly Powers unite with him; they occupy the entire space around the altar, to honor Him who lies there as a Sacrifice.[132]

---

[130] See Scheeben, *The Mysteries of Christianity,* 507; Gihr, *The Holy Sacrifice of the Mass,* 697–699.

[131] Pope St. Gregory the Great (*Dial.* IV, 58), as cited in Gihr, *The Holy Sacrifice of the Mass,* 702; see CCC 1137–1139, 1326.

[132] St. John Chrysostom ("Of the Priesthood," VI, 4), as cited in Gihr, *The Holy Sacrifice of the Mass,* 697–698; the angels honor

While we can gain a better understanding of the Sacrifice of the Mass, clarifying what it is and what it is not, we must also ultimately realize that the best human attempts to explain this glorious and divine mystery will always fall short. As one liturgist in the Middle Ages observed, "These words of mystery are so profound, so wonderful and inconceivable ... that we ought rather to revere them with humility and a holy awe than attempt to interpret them."[133] In other words, we must bow before the mystery and thank God for the incomparable blessing of participating in the Mass. For "by the Eucharistic celebration we already unite ourselves with the heavenly liturgy and anticipate eternal life, when God will be all in all" (CCC 1326; see 1 Cor. 15:28).

Bodily Present in Heaven and in the Blessed Sacrament: The Miracle of the Eucharist

While the Mass is indeed ultimately a divine mystery, a crucial issue remains to be addressed to make the biblical story of the Mass more understandable to both Catholics and non-Catholics alike. No Christian doubts that Christ can be everywhere *as a divine Person*. But we understandably struggle more when we try to imagine his *limited* human body in more than one place at one time. If Christ is present in his glorified body in the heavenly sanctuary, ministering as a priest forever, how can he be bodily present anywhere else, since he has only one glorified, albeit finite, body?

Christ, who, although bearing the marks of having been slain, stands triumphantly (see Rev. 5:5–14).

[133] Gihr, *The Holy Sacrifice of the Mass*, 701, footnote omitted.

The answer goes to the heart of the Eucharistic Mystery, which is often referred to simply as "the mystery par excellence."[134] A divine mystery is a truth that we, humanly speaking, will never be able to comprehend fully. It is a truth so big that we cannot wrap our minds all the way around it. We can grasp it somewhat with our reason, but a divine mystery inevitably transcends — not contradicts — our ability to understand. In addition, we must recognize that the Eucharistic Mystery is an extension of another mystery: the Incarnation, in which the divine Son of God assumed a human nature when Mary conceived him by the power of the Holy Spirit (see CCC 456, 461–463, 484–486). His being a divine Person with two natures — one divine and one human — is known as the "hypostatic union" (see CCC 464–469), and this explains why we call Jesus the God-man.

In his divinity, Christ is omnipotent (all powerful), omniscient (all knowing), and omnipresent (everywhere). The *Catechism* affirms God's and thus Christ's omnipresence (no. 2671), as does Sacred Scripture (Deut. 4:39; Matt. 5:35; 6:9–10; Acts 17:24–28). In his divine essence, Jesus is a pure spirit. He is wholly present in an undivided manner everywhere. In his divine essence, therefore, Jesus has no parts, although he did take on a human nature at his Incarnation. By way of comparison, we as human persons are by nature body-soul composites (see CCC 362–368). Our bodies have parts but our souls, as created spirits, do not have parts. Thus, each person's soul animates (enlivens) his body and is present throughout his body in a whole and undivided manner. How a spirit functions in relation to a body

---

[134] Scheeben, *The Mysteries of Christianity*, 469. See also the treatment of St. Thomas Aquinas on this issue in his *Summa Theologica*, III, Q. 76.

will be an important concept to keep in mind when considering the mystery of the Eucharist.

Now let us reflect on Christ's human nature. By virtue of his triumphant Resurrection, Christ attained "a glorified body: not limited by space and time but able to be present how and when he wills" (CCC 645). Thus, Jesus is able to walk through closed doors (John 20:26) and make sudden appearances at will (Luke 24:36). St. Paul calls the resurrected body a "spiritual body" (1 Cor. 15:44). We too will have glorified bodies when we rise at the resurrection of the dead at the end of the world (CCC 999). However, what takes place in the miracle of the Eucharist is something far more profound. First, we must recognize that, given its limited human nature, Christ's body cannot be in more than one place *by the power of that same human nature*. In other words, a limited human body can never be in more than one place by virtue of its own *human* power. In addition, being joined to Christ's divine Person via the Incarnation does not mean that his human nature will thereby automatically partake of his divine power to be present throughout the world. But the Incarnation does make wondrous things possible for Christ's Body, Blood, and Soul—namely, the Sacrament of the Eucharist.

So how does Christ become present in the Eucharist around the world and yet remain in heaven? While his body never ceases to be human, let us first consider that Christ enables it to be present after the manner of a spirit in the Eucharist. That is, Christ is present in the Eucharistic elements as our human souls are diffused throughout our bodies: in a whole and undivided manner. Jesus' body remains a body, but, like a spirit, his body becomes miraculously present in a whole and undivided manner in each and every Eucharistic Host, and thus in each and every part of each Host. The *Catechism* (no. 1377) affirms this mystery:

> The Eucharistic presence of Christ begins at the moment of the consecration and endures as long as the Eucharistic species subsist. Christ is present whole and entire in each of their parts, in such a way that the breaking of the bread does not divide Christ [cf. Council of Trent: DS 1641].[135]

In addition, while the "substance" or essential matter of bread and wine is transubstantiated[136] into the Body and Blood

[135] In canon 3 of the Council of Trent's "Canons on the Most Holy Sacrament of the Eucharist," the Church provides, "If anyone denies that in the venerable sacrament of the Eucharist the whole Christ is contained under each form [that is, bread and wine] and under every part of each form when separated, let him be anathema," as cited in *Canons and Decrees of the Council of Trent*, 79, footnote omitted.

[136] In his 1965 encyclical on the Eucharist, *Mysterium Fidei* ("The Mystery of Faith"), Pope Paul VI concisely affirms "the dogma of transubstantiation" (no. 10; see no. 24; as given at http://www.vatican.va; see also Pope John Paul II's 2003 encyclical *Ecclesia de Eucharistia*, no. 9). "For what now lies beneath the aforementioned species is not what was there before," writes the Pope, "but something completely different; and not just in the estimation of Church belief but in reality, since once the substance or nature of the bread and wine has been changed into the body and blood of Christ, nothing remains of the bread and the wine except for the species—beneath which Christ is present whole and entire in His physical 'reality,' corporeally present, although not in the manner in which bodies are in a place" (Paul VI, *Mysterium Fidei*, no. 46). In saying "not in the manner in which bodies are in a place," the Pope means not in the way bodies are normally present. Rather, as explained above, Christ's Body is present in the Eucharist after the manner of a spirit.

of Christ, the "accidents"[137] of bread and wine, that is, the color, taste, appearance and feel, miraculously remain (see CCC 1376–1377). Normally, if a thing's substance is withdrawn from existence, its accidents would naturally perish with it.[138] But the accidents of the bread and wine are kept in existence because Jesus gives his body the divine power to coexist with them. That is, Jesus wills his body to go beyond its limited human nature and become a participant in his divine attributes. In addition, Christ's body does not become omnipresent through the Sacrament of the Eucharist, but Christ omnipotently enables his body to have "a share" in his divine omnipresence. Specifically, Jesus enables his body to become sacramentally present wherever the Mass is celebrated and wherever he — our Eucharistic Lord — is reposed in a tabernacle or worshipped in adoration. Fr. Scheeben helps make the Eucharistic Mystery more accessible:

> Because the body of Christ is the body of the Son of God, it receives through the power of the divine person inhabiting it the unique privilege, similar to the prerogative of the person Himself, but in limited measure, of being

---

[137] Accidents are things that by nature are required to exist in another being or thing. Accidents are also known as attributes or qualities or properties of someone or something, For example, you never see a "blue." It's always a blue coat or a blue car or something else blue. In the Eucharist, while the substance of wine no longer exists, for example, the various properties of wine continue to exist, including its color, taste, and power potentially to intoxicate. For an excellent primer on accidents in light of the Church's teaching on the Eucharist, see Frank J. Sheed's *Theology for Beginners* (Ann Arbor, MI: Servant Books, 1982), 156–158.

[138] Scheeben, *The Mysteries of Christianity*, 474.

present indivisible and undivided in many places and in the innermost recesses of things. Not formally through the hypostatic union, but still because of it and on the basis of it, the Son of God raises the body He has assumed to a share in the simplicity, universality, and pervasive power of His divine existence.[139]

"But," some might protest, "that's humanly impossible!" Exactly. For a human person, such a wondrous action is indeed impossible. But when a human body was united to a *divine* Person at the Incarnation, the miracle of the Eucharist became a possibility, for "all things are possible with God" (Matt. 19:26). Again, as Fr. Scheeben notes, Christ's body does not automatically (or "formally") partake of his divine powers simply by being united to his divine nature. But the hypostatic union does create the possibility that Jesus can make the Sacrament of the Eucharist a reality, that he can will it into existence. After all, if Jesus can take on a human nature, mysteriously becoming fully human while remaining fully divine, is not providing the Eucharist *also* possible for such an omnipotent God? Fr. Scheeben summarizes the implications and consequences of the Eucharistic miracle for Christ's body:

> The substance of Christ's body exists in a way that is not natural to it, but supernatural to it. We cannot form a direct concept, but only an analogous one of this supernatural mode of existence. For to form a concept of the mode of existence of Christ's body in the Eucharist, we must transfer it to our notions of the natural existence of other substances [namely, created spirits and the

---

[139] Ibid., 476.

uncreated God]. Herein precisely is the miracle and the mystery: in the Eucharist the body of Christ exists supernaturally in a way that only substances of an entirely different kind can exist naturally [again, Fr. Scheeben refers to created spirits and the uncreated God]. Although material in itself, the body of Christ exists after the fashion of a spiritual substance, so far as, like the soul in the body, it is substantially present whole and indivisible in the entire host and in every part of it, and is beyond all sensible perception. Moreover, the existence of the body of Christ in the Eucharist is analogous to the existence of the divine substance. That is, it exists in a way that is naturally impossible even to a created spiritual substance, since it is present not only in a single place, but in numberless separate places ... wherever the [Eucharistic] bread is consecrated.[140]

The concept is admittedly not a simple one, but Christ helps us understand the Eucharistic miracle through his other miracles, specifically the multiplication of loaves and fish discussed in the first part of John 6. Some Christians who affirm this miracle will nevertheless argue that the crowd ate many *different* loaves. Yet, we must remember that the many loaves that fed thousands had their origin in a *mere five loaves*. That is, Christ temporarily suspended the laws of physics and divinely "stretched" the five loaves to become many loaves, so that the crowd could be fed. If Christ can do that with regular bread, why can't he do something much more extraordinary with his glorified body so

---

[140] Scheeben, *The Mysteries of Christianity*, 470–471, 473, emphasis added.

that the world can be fed supernaturally? Some may not believe in the Eucharist, but Catholic apologist Karl Keating notes that they should not argue that the omnipotent God is incapable of making the sacrament:

> If Christ, who was on earth in a natural body and now reigns in heaven in a glorified body, can make the world out of nothing, certainly he can make bread and wine into his own Body and Blood. That should not be hard to accept, no matter how hard it might be to fathom. There is no good reason to limit God's acts to the extent of our understanding.[141]

In his encyclical *Ecclesia de Eucharistia,* Pope John Paul II asserts that the Blessed Mother would argue similarly:

> With the same maternal concern which she showed at the wedding feast of Cana, Mary seems to say to us: "Do not waver; trust in the words of my Son, If he was able to change water into wine, he can also turn bread and wine into his body and blood, and through this mystery

---

[141] Keating, *Catholicism and Fundamentalism,* 243. Keating's argument echoes the Council of Trent, which provides, "For there is no repugnance in this that our Savior sits always at the right hand of the Father in heaven according to the natural mode of existing, and yet is in many other places sacramentally present to us in His own substance by a manner of existence which, though we can scarcely express in words, yet with our understanding illumined by faith we can conceive and ought most firmly to believe is possible to God" (Council of Trent, "Decree Concerning the Most Holy Sacrament of the Eucharist," chap. 1, as cited in *Canons and Decrees of the Council of Trent,* 73, footnotes omitted).

bestow on believers the living memorial of his passover, thus becoming the 'bread of life.'"[142]

Fr. Scheeben sheds further light on the Eucharistic miracle by means of an analogy. As a single thought can become present to many people through the means of sound waves, so too God himself can be distributed through the means of Eucharistic Hosts at Mass. Here Scheeben cites the work of Guitmund of Aversa, an eleventh-century bishop and theologian:

We are aware from everyday experience that our thought, that is, the word of our mind, can in a certain way be clothed with sound, so that the thought which was concealed in our mind and was known to us alone can be uttered, and thus manifested to others. Even while it remains wholly in our own mind, it can be wholly made known to a thousand persons through the agency of the sound it has assumed, so that it not only simultaneously illuminates the minds of them all, but at the same time, still whole and entire, strikes the ears of all with the sound in which it is embodied. If, then, God has conferred such power on the human word that not only the word itself, but the sound wherewith it is it clothed, can at the same time reach a thousand people without any cleavage of its being, no one ought to refuse to believe the same, even if he cannot understand it, of the only and omnipotent and co-eternal word of the omnipotent Father, and of the flesh in which He is clothed, so that the Word Himself may be known to us [in the Eucharist]. Neither can we understand the matter as regards the tenuous and fleeting

[142] John Paul II, *Ecclesia de Eucharistia,* no. 54.

word of a man, and the sounds which scarcely hover in existence for a second, and yet we accept it on the basis of daily experience.[143]

Scheeben wrote in the late nineteenth century, before the invention of radio and television. The analogy he cites becomes even more compelling when we consider the worldwide impact that broadcast technology can have on a single, uttered word.

In summary, the body of Christ can be both in heaven and on earth because the omnipotent Christ wills it so for our salvific benefit. While Christ's human body is limited in itself, it can share in God's divine power by Christ's willing that it do so.

Pope Paul VI provides an appropriate summary for our extensive discussion. In *Credo of the People of God*, a solemn profession of faith published in 1968, the pope weaves together the various lessons of this chapter in a profoundly succinct fashion:

We believe that the Mass, celebrated by the priest representing the person of Christ by virtue of the power received through the Sacrament of Orders, and offered by him in the name of Christ and the members of His Mystical Body, is in true reality the sacrifice of Calvary, rendered sacramentally present on our altars. We believe that as the bread and wine consecrated by the Lord at the Last Supper were changed into His body and His blood which were to be offered for us on the cross, likewise the bread and wine consecrated by the priest are changed into the body and blood of Christ enthroned gloriously in heaven, and we believe that the mysterious presence of

---

[143] Scheeben, *The Mysteries of Christianity*, 515–516.

the Lord, under what continues to appear to our senses as before, is a true, real and substantial presence (no. 24).[144]

"Thy kingdom come. Thy will be done, on earth as it is in heaven." As we have seen in various ways, nowhere are those words of the Lord's Prayer more profoundly fulfilled than in the Sacrifice of the Mass.

Questions for Reflection and Discussion

1. (a) Explain why Christ's Sacrifice does not appear to fit into traditional Jewish sacrificial categories. (b) What New Testament evidence conveys that Christ's Self-Sacrifice fulfilled a unique Old Testament prophecy about sacrifice— namely Isaiah's suffering servant?

2. Scripture says that Jesus had to be "perfected" in offering his Sacrifice and then offer that Sacrifice to the Father in heaven to perfect us. (a) How was Christ perfected? (b) How does Christ perfect us? Stated another way, what scriptural evidence would you provide to demonstrate that Christ's Sacrifice did not begin and end on the Cross, and that his Ascension was indispensable in securing our redemption and providing us with the opportunity for eternal salvation?

3. (a) According to the material presented in this chapter, why might Hebrews 5:7–10 be called the most profound scriptural passage in the biblical story of the Mass? (b) How does

---

[144] Pope Paul VI, *Credo of the People of God*, in Msgr. Eugene Kevane, ed., *Teaching the Catholic Faith Today: Twentieth Century Catechetical Documents of the Holy See* (Boston: Daughters of St. Paul, 102), 37.

Christ exercise his Melchizedekian priesthood to make his perpetual, heavenly Sacrifice present and thereby fulfill the New Covenant Passover ordinance?

4. For those Christians who do not believe the Mass is a Sacrifice, what biblical questions, particularly in light of Christ's Melchizedekian priesthood, can Catholics raise as a witness to them?

5. Jesus is a "priest for ever according to the order of Melchizedek," yet "for ever" in this case can mean "until the end of time" or "everlasting," that is, without end. Explain how Jesus' one Sacrifice will be offered in one Melchizedekian manner until the end of time, that is, until his Second Coming, and in another Melchizedekian manner without end, that is, for all eternity.

6. (a) How would you respond to charges that asking the Father to accept our Sacrifice at Mass is an offense against Christ? That is, why does the Church ask the Father to accept our Sacrifice at Mass? (b) Explain the proper understanding of the prayer at Mass "[A]lmighty God, command that these gifts be borne by the hands of your holy Angel to your altar on high."

7. (a) Explain how Christ can be bodily present in heaven, while simultaneously also being present in a bodily manner on earth in the Sacrament of the Eucharist? (b) How does the miracle of the loaves support the Church's teaching? (c) What analogy does Fr. Scheeben use to convey the sacramental reality that Christ can be bodily present wherever the Mass is celebrated?

8. How would you argue that the Sacrifice of the Mass most profoundly fulfills the words of the Lord's Prayer, "Thy kingdom come. Thy will be done, on earth as it is heaven"?

13

"Proclaiming the Lord's
Death until He Comes"
The Mass in the Early Church and Beyond

Background Reading
    Luke 24:1–35
    1 Corinthians 10:1–22
    1 Corinthians 11:17–34
    Acts 20:7–12
    Hebrews 13

Jesus came to fulfill the law and the prophets, not to abolish them (Matt. 5:17). Nowhere is this fact clearer than in the establishment of the Mass. The Old Covenant was inaugurated with the shedding of blood (Exod. 24:1–11), and Jesus followed in a similar ritual, shedding his own blood on Calvary, the blood of the new and everlasting Covenant (see Luke 22:20–21; Jer. 31:31–34). In establishing the New Covenant, Jesus instituted a memorial that sacramentally re-presents the very same Sacrifice of Calvary, a Sacrifice that "completes and surpasses all the sacrifices of the Old Covenant" (CCC 1330), including the Passover and Day of Atonement offerings, as well as the Tamid lamb sacrifices. Jesus died only once in history; but his Sacrifice of Calvary culminated in everlasting glory in heaven, as the worthy "Lamb standing, as though it had been slain," wondrously attests (Rev. 5:6; see Heb. 7:23–25; 9:24).

There are several post-Resurrection passages in the New Testament that provide support for the institution of the Mass. For example, on that first Easter Sunday, two disciples participated in what Christian tradition commonly holds was the first liturgy after Jesus rose from the dead.[145] Jesus had risen, word of his Resurrection was getting around, and then our Lord came upon two disciples as they traveled to Emmaus, an ancient town west of Jerusalem. The disciples did not immediately recognize Jesus, perhaps because of his glorified body, and they were exasperated that Jesus had apparently not heard about the events of recent days, including the alleged Resurrection of a Nazarene whom many had hoped would redeem Israel:

> And he [Jesus] said to them, "O foolish men, and slow of heart to believe all that the prophets have spoken! Was it not necessary that the Christ [that is, the Messiah] should suffer these things and enter into his glory?" And beginning with Moses and all the prophets, he interpreted to them in all the scriptures the things concerning himself. (Luke 24:25–27)

Jesus' disciples had embraced the glorious aspects of the Messiah, but not the more difficult. Jesus had foretold his death, that he was called to lay down his life for their redemption (see Luke 22:37), yet most of his disciples deserted him at Calvary. On the road to Emmaus, he surely expounded on how he was

[145] See page 20, n. 17.

the suffering-servant Lamb, who came to take away the sins of the world, fulfilling the Day of Atonement Sacrifice. Given that "he interpreted to them in *all the scriptures the things concerning himself*" (Luke 24:27, emphasis added), it would seem logical that Jesus would have explained more fully to the pair what he had originally told his twelve apostles at the Last Supper: that the Passover would henceforth be a remembrance of his Sacrifice. Nevertheless, it was only in the subsequent "breaking of the bread" that the two disciples finally recognized Jesus.

"Breaking of bread" was a ritual action among Jewish families at the beginning of their meals, in which the father took bread, blessed it, broke it, and gave it to his family. The blessing was crucial: "It showed that those present were receiving from God the food needed for their life; the food was thereby drawn into the current of divine power."[146] Jesus adapted this rite in transforming the Passover at the Last Supper, using the fourfold action of taking, blessing, breaking, and giving, an action he similarly repeated with the two disciples on the road to Emmaus (Luke 24:30). As CCC 1329 provides,

> It is by this action [breaking of the bread] that his disciples will recognize him after his Resurrection [cf. Luke 24:13–35], and it is this expression that the first Christians will use to designate their Eucharistic assemblies [cf. Acts 2:42, 46; 20:7, 11]; by doing so they signified that all who eat the one broken bread, Christ, enter into communion with him and form but one body in him [cf. 1 Cor 10:16–17].

As the events near Emmaus appear to illustrate, Jesus enacted in sequence what has been the structure of the Eucharistic liturgy

---

[146] Léon-Dufour, S.J., *Sharing the Eucharistic Bread*, 22.

ever since: the liturgy of the Word, that is, the reading and explanation of the Scriptures; and the liturgy of the Eucharist, that is, the offering and consuming of the sacramental Sacrifice (CCC 1346–1347). This fundamental, two-part liturgical structure, in which Christ is encountered in both word and sacrament, serves as a template for sacramental communion with the risen Jesus in general. It constitutes "one single act of worship"[147] and can be seen elsewhere in the Bible, such as in the Mass that St. Paul celebrated in Troas, a small town on the northwest coast of present-day Turkey (Acts 20:7–12).

As if to emphasize the sacramental nature of Jesus' actions, Luke concludes the Emmaus road passage by saying that the disciples came to know Jesus in "the breaking of the bread" (24:35). When his disciples recognize him, Jesus vanishes, as if to say that he is still present in the Eucharistic Bread and therefore his visible presence need not continue. Similarly, he calls us to have faith in his sacramental Presence in the Mass today.

One Bread, One Body

In his first letter to the Corinthians, St. Paul provides an excellent catechesis on the Mass, demonstrating again that it is not a simple memorial, but an actual Sacrifice. After telling the Corinthians that God will not allow them to be tempted beyond their strength and will provide them a way to escape temptations (1 Cor. 10:12–13), Paul provides that the way involves partaking of the Eucharistic Sacrifice and avoiding idolatrous worship:

---

[147] Vatican II, *Sacrosanctum Concilium* ("Constitution on the Sacred Liturgy"), no. 56, as cited in Flannery, *Vatican Council II*, 19.

Therefore, my beloved, shun the worship of idols. I speak as to sensible men; judge for yourselves what I say. The cup of blessing which we bless, is it not a participation in the blood of Christ? The bread which we break, is it not a participation in the body of Christ? Because there is one bread, we who are many are one body, for we all partake of the one bread. (1 Cor. 10:14–17)

Notice first that Paul does not seek to persuade with extensive arguments that the bread and wine truly become the Body and Blood of Jesus, which the faithful receive as Holy Communion. Rather, his rhetorical questions expect affirmative answers. That is, he assumes the Christians in Corinth already understand and believe in the Eucharist. As in 1 Corinthians 11:23–27, Paul's concise presentation conveys that the Real Presence is accepted fact,[148] and he, as a good teacher, is reaffirming important lessons. Holy Communion unites the faithful more closely to Christ and, in receiving his Body and Blood, they are also united by Christ more closely to each other in his Mystical Body, the Church: "Communion renews, strengthens, and deepens this incorporation into the Church, already achieved by Baptism" (CCC 1396).

After matter-of-factly affirming Christ's Real Presence in the Eucharist, Paul explains how we are able to eat his Flesh and drink his Blood: this New Covenant celebration is indeed a Communion Sacrifice. Most Protestant apologists counter that "the Lord's supper" (1 Cor. 11:20) is only a symbolic recalling of the Last Supper, not a sacrificial re-presentation, because Paul

---

[148] W. Rees, "1 and 2 Corinthians," in Dom Bernard Orchard et al., *A Catholic Commentary on Holy Scripture* (New York: Thomas Nelson and Sons, 1953), 1094, no. 878g.

tells the Corinthians that they should not partake of both the "table" (Greek: *trapeza*) of demons and that of the Lord (1 Cor. 10:21). If Paul had wanted to convey that the Eucharist is actually a sacrifice, they argue, he would have instead used the Greek word for "altar," that is, *thusiasterion* ("place of sacrifice"),[149] which he uses in reference to Israel's altar of sacrifice in the Temple (1 Cor. 10:18).

Biblical context, though, is crucial. *Table* can mean "altar" if the context is clearly a sacrificial one. Paul makes unmistakably clear in his analogy in 1 Corinthians 10 that he is talking about eating things that have been sacrificed. First, as noted, he speaks of Israel's altar of sacrifice in the Temple: "[A]re not those who eat the *sacrifices* partners in the *altar?*" (1 Cor. 10:18, emphasis added). Second, one should not presume a nonsacrificial meaning regarding the New Covenant "table of the Lord" (1 Cor. 10:21) just because Paul does not use *thusiasterion*. Why? Because, in discussing the Old Covenant altar of sacrifice located in the Temple, the prophet Malachi interchangeably refers to this altar as both an "altar" (Mal. 1:7, 10) and "the Lord's table" (Mal. 1:7, 12). Again, context is crucial.

Consider further that Paul notes that the Corinthians will become "partners with demons" (1 Cor. 10:20) — entering into communion with the henchmen of the devil, the mystical body of Satan — if they eat something that has been offered to idols. To sacrifice to an idol and partake of the sacrifice, Paul says, is

---

[149] Paul R. McReynolds, *Word Study Greek-English New Testament* (Wheaton, IL: Tyndale House, 1998), 619, 818. See also Spiros Zodhiates, ed., *The Hebrew-Greek Key Study Bible*, New American Standard Bible version (Chattanooga, TN: AMG Publishers, 1990), 72, no. 5132 and 37, no. 2379, respectively, of the "Greek Dictionary of the New Testament" appendix.

necessarily to serve Satan, because the true object of devotion behind every stone or metal idol is the devil, who inspired its construction. Paul adds that Christians should consequently not provoke God (1 Cor. 10:22), alluding to the judgment ancient Israel endured when it provoked Yahweh with its own idolatrous practices (see also Deut. 32:15ff.).

Had Paul wanted to distinguish sharply between the actual sacrifices offered in the Temple and to demons, on one hand, and the merely symbolic meal of the Eucharist, on the other, he would have made a clearer distinction. He would have made sure that the Corinthians did not misunderstand his sacrificial analogy and erroneously conclude that the Eucharist is a genuine sacrifice. Instead, Paul teaches in a quite contrary manner. First he emphasizes that the Eucharist *is* the Body and Blood of Jesus (1 Cor. 10:14–17) and then proceeds to compare the sacrificial nature of the Eucharist with other contemporary sacrificial meals — that is, communion sacrifices. Paul dwells on the peril of consuming demonic sacrifices, not on clarifying alleged sacrificial misunderstandings regarding the Eucharist.

"The New Covenant in My Blood"

Paul continues his discussion of the Mass in the next chapter,[150] chastising the Corinthians for their irreverent manner in approaching the Eucharist (1 Cor. 11:17–22). He calls the Mass "the Lord's supper" (11:20), the only time the expression is used in the New Testament and a reminder that what Christians celebrate in the liturgy is intimately connected with the Last Supper, the New Covenant Passover. Paul says that the Corinthians' irreverence

---

[150] Dividing biblical books into chapters is actually a later addition that the Catholic Church implemented.

is rooted in a fellowship meal they eat before the liturgy begins; some Corinthians are failing to share with the poor and some are even becoming drunk (11:21). Paul chastises the Corinthians because these sins profane their participation in the sacred celebration of Mass, which immediately followed the fellowship meal. Paul emphasizes that the Mass is a sublime "remembrance" of the Last Supper and thus the Sacrifice of Calvary (11:23–26; see CCC 1356–1358). Paul further conveys that the Eucharist is the fulfillment of the biblical story of the Mass, because Christ said it is "the new covenant in my blood" (11:25) and, as Paul adds, "as often as you eat this bread and drink the cup, you proclaim the Lord's death until he comes" (11:26; see CCC 1344 and 1356).

Given its sublime nature, Paul cautions that irreverent reception of the Eucharist makes one guilty of "profaning the body and blood of the Lord," and that is why, the apostle adds, some have gotten sick and even died (11:27–30). The Mass is a solemn ritual in which the Church not only collectively renews its covenant with Christ, but also each individual disciple intimately renews his personal covenant commitment with the Lord as a member of his Mystical Body. To receive the Lord in an unworthy manner — that is, in a state of mortal sin — calls down the judgment of God, much as an adulterous husband does in resuming conjugal relations with his wife without first repenting of his infidelity (see CCC 1385). One could not profane Christ's Body and Blood if the Eucharist were simply common bread and wine (or grape juice), nor would death result. Paul's sobering words on the Eucharist and the irreverent reception thereof testify, again, to the Real Presence. The divine punishments associated with irreverently receiving Communion are intended to be remedial, not ultimately condemnatory (11:32), yet Christians in mortal sin should not receive the Eucharist, lest they magnify their sin by profaning Christ (see Heb. 10:26–31). For the Corinthians, the grave sins were partaking of Christ in a state of drunkenness and doing so after discriminating against the poor who had nothing to eat at the fellowship meal. Paul reminds us that membership has not only its privileges but also its grave responsibilities.

The Lord's Day Fulfills the Sabbath: Covenant Transition in the Early Church

As the Mass has fulfilled the Passover and other Old Covenant sacrifices, Sunday (the Lord's Day) has fulfilled the Sabbath as the Third Commandment day of rest and worship of God (CCC 2175–2176). The Lord's Day gets its name because Jesus rose from the dead on Sunday (CCC 2174). Because Christ instituted the Mass as "the memorial of his death and Resurrection" (CCC 1337), and because Sunday has fulfilled the Sabbath, Catholics are obligated to participate in Mass on Sunday. The Sabbath is the last day of the week, running from sundown Friday to sundown Saturday, while the Lord's Day traditionally began on Saturday evening. In his travels to Troas (Acts 20:7–12), Paul celebrated Mass on the first day of the week — that is, after sundown Saturday, following the Jewish custom of measuring days (see Lev. 23:32) — and he thereby provided a precedent for the Church to allow Saturday vigil Masses today. The liturgy began with the Word of God, including an extended sermon by Paul that continued until midnight. After miraculously raising Eutychus from the dead, Paul culminated the Mass with the breaking of the bread (Acts 20:11), that is, the liturgy of the Eucharist, although he stayed on to converse until dawn.

The earliest Christian writings after the Bible affirm that the Lord's Day fulfilled the Sabbath and that the celebration of the

Eucharist had become its focus. In his *Letter to the Magnesians* (c. A.D. 110), St. Ignatius of Antioch teaches that "those who were brought up in the ancient order of things have come to the possession of a new hope, no longer observing the Sabbath, but living in the observance of the Lords' Day, on which also our life has sprung up again by Him and by His death."[151] A longer, edited version of the same letter describes the Lord's Day as "the resurrection-day, the queen and chief of all the days [of the week]."[152]

Another early Church writing was the *Didache* (Greek for "Teaching"), which purports to be the "Teaching of the Twelve Apostles" and was written in the first or second century. The *Didache* not only teaches that the Mass — "the breaking of the bread" — had become the focus of Lord's Day worship in the early Church, but it also uses the word *sacrifice* a total of four times to describe the nature of the sacramental celebration. For example, the *Didache* provides:

> On the Lord's Day ... gather together, break bread and give thanks, after confessing your transgressions so that your sacrifice may be pure.... For this is that which was proclaimed by the Lord: "In every place and time let there be offered to Me a clean sacrifice...." (see Mal. 1:11)[153]

---

[151] Ignatius of Antioch, *Letter to the Magnesians* (shorter version), 9, 1, as cited in Alexander Roberts and James Donaldson, *Ante-Nicene Fathers* (Peabody, MA: Hendrickson Publishers, 1994), 1:62; see CCC 2175.

[152] Ignatius of Antioch, *Letter to the Magnesians* (longer version), 9, as cited in Roberts and Donaldson, *Ante-Nicene Fathers*, 1:63.

[153] *Didache*, 14, 1 and 3, as cited in William A. Jurgens, *The Faith of the Early Fathers*, no. 8 (Collegeville, MN: Liturgical Press, 1970), 1:4.

"Proclaiming the Lord's Death until He Comes"

The early Church clearly taught that the Eucharist is indeed a sacrifice involving Christ's Body and Blood, and St. Justin Martyr (c. A.D. 155)[154] and St. Irenaeus (c. A.D. 199)[155] both affirmed that the Eucharist fulfills the prophesied sacrifice of Malachi 1:11.

The *Didache* also affirms the meal aspect of the New Covenant Passover, echoing Christ's words that we should seek food that is not perishable but rather imperishable, for his Body and Blood are real food and drink that provide eternal life (see John 6:54–55):

> You, almighty Master, have created all things for your name's sake, and have given food and drink to men for their enjoyment, so that they might return thanks to you. Upon us, however, you have bestowed spiritual food and drink, and eternal life through your Servant.[156]

The generation following Christ's Resurrection was a transitional time of "covenant overlap," because Jewish Christians worshipped God at both the Temple (see Luke 24:53; Acts 2:46) and on the Lord's Day in the Mass. Yet those who clung to the Old Covenant exclusively could not partake of the Body and Blood of Christ. Making reference to Temple priests in terms that hearkened back to Israel's wilderness tabernacle, the Letter to the Hebrews says, "We have an altar from which those who serve the tent have no right to eat" (Heb. 13:10). The Greek word used in Hebrews 13:10 is *thusiasterion*, which, as noted earlier, is

---

[154] St. Justin Martyr, *Dialogue with Trypho*, 41, as cited in Jurgens, *Faith of the Early Fathers*, no. 135, 1:60.

[155] St. Irenaeus, *Against Heresies*, 4, 17, 5, as cited in Jurgens, *Faith of the Early Fathers*, no. 232, 1:95.

[156] *Didache*, 10, 3, as cited in Jurgens, *Faith of the Early Fathers*, no. 7, 1:3.

a "place of sacrifice." The Letter to the Hebrews conveys that a real altar of sacrifice is used in the New Covenant, an altar on which the Church not only offers sacrifice but also partakes of that which is offered. This is further evidence that the Mass is the fulfilled New Covenant Passover.

For those who insist on a figurative interpretation of *altar* in Hebrews 13:10: is the food that the Old Covenant priests have no right to eat also figurative, as if the Letter to the Hebrews only means "consuming" God's Word? The passage makes little sense if one assumes a figurative interpretation, and, indeed, the context of the passage indicates a literal reading is intended by the author. When considered in the additional light of other Eucharistic passages in the New Testament, the strongly liturgical nature of the Letter to the Hebrews in general, and other overwhelming evidence from the early Church testifying to the reality of the Eucharist, a merely figurative reading of Hebrews 13:10 cannot be credibly sustained.

And who may partake of this Sacrifice? Because of Christ's universal atonement, everyone is welcome but membership is gained by accepting God's saving invitation, not through ancestral pedigree and undergoing outdated rituals. As St. Paul teaches elsewhere, all become one in Christ, beginning in Baptism:

> For as many of you as were baptized into Christ have put on Christ. There is neither Jew nor Greek, there is neither slave nor free, there is neither male nor female; for you are all one in Christ Jesus. And if you are Christ's, *then you are Abraham's offspring, heirs according to promise* (Gal. 3:27–29, emphasis added; see Gen. 22:14; Matt. 1:1).

In addition, the equality of Christians does not preclude a supreme, visible, human authority. Both in the Old and New

Covenants, God provides human authorities to guide his people, beginning with Moses in the Old and Peter, the first Pope, in the New.[157] In the New Covenant, Christ mediates his "full authority" through the leaders of his Church, who teach and govern in his name (Matt. 28:18–20; see John 20:21). Christians are called to be obedient: "Obey your leaders and submit to them; for they are keeping watch over your souls, as men who will have to give account. Let them do this joyfully, and not sadly, for that would be of no advantage to you" (Heb. 13:17). Of course, as men called to be faithful servant-shepherds of Christ, Church leaders have to be accountable to both God and their flocks.

Divinely Planned Obsolescence:
Temple Sacrifices Give Way to the Mass

The heart of Old Covenant worship ended abruptly and violently in A.D. 70, when the Romans destroyed Jerusalem and its Temple. The Temple had fulfilled its prefiguring purpose in salvation history, and its destruction by the Romans within a generation of Christ's Ascension sorrowfully fulfilled Christ's prophecy that this primary feature of Old Covenant worship would come to a dramatic end (see Matt. 24:1–2; see CCC 839–840). Almost three hundred years later, the Roman emperor Julian set out to refute Christ and his New Covenant. He had developed a burning hatred of Christianity, apparently initiated at age six, when a previous Christian emperor had directed the killing of most of the male members of his family. The young lad would go on

---

[157] To read more on this subject, see CUF's FAITH FACTS "That They May All Be One" and "Rock Solid." They are free and available online at http://www.cuf.org, or by calling CUF toll-free at (800) MY-FAITH (693-2484).

to repudiate Catholicism and thus became known in history as Julian the Apostate. As emperor, Julian decided to discredit Jesus Christ and his Catholic Church once and for all. His plan? Rebuild the Temple and reinstitute its Old Covenant sacrifices, thus nullifying Christ's words in Matthew 24:1–2. The "gates of hell" would thereby prevail not only against Christ's Church (see Matt. 16:18) but against Christ himself.

As one historian describes the emperor's attempt, "The high priest of the Hellenes would embarrass the God of the Galileans on His own terrain, making Him out to be a charlatan."[158] The Church could do nothing but invoke God's aid. How many divisions does the Pope have? A rather omnipotent army of One, as Julian would learn. Historian Giuseppe Ricciotti retells the dramatic story as it unfolded:

> After he made his decision, Julian entrusted its execution to Alypius, a trustworthy individual.... The events which followed would be almost incredible if they were not attested with substantial agreement by Julian's pagan friend Ammianus (23.1.2ff), by the Arian Philostorgius (7.9), and by orthodox Christians such as Rufinus (I.37–39), Socrates (3.20), Sozomen (5.22), Theodoret (3.15), [and the Church Father] Gregory Nazianzen (5.3–8)[159]

---

[158] Giuseppe Ricciotti, *Julian the Apostate*, trans. M. Joseph Costelloe, S.J. (Milwaukee: Bruce Publishing, 1960), 224.

[159] Ibid. Ricciotti's references are to the following ancient works: Ammianus Marcellinus, *Rerum gestarum libri* (Loeb Classical Library [LCL]); Philostorgius, *Historia ecclesiastica* (*Patrologia Graecae* [PG] 65); Rufinus, *Historic ecclsiastica* (*Patrologia Latina* [PL] 21); Socrates, *Historia ecclesiastica* (PG 67); Sozomen, *Historia ecclesiastica* (PG 67); Theodoret, *Historia ecclesiatica*

and others.... According to Ammianus, Julian allotted enormous sums for the enterprise....

Toward the close of 362, however, violent earthquakes occurred along the Palestinian coast [and elsewhere].... Jerusalem also suffered from these great tremors. Recently cleared portions of the temple area were at times littered with ruins caused by the earthquakes. On one occasion a violent tremor caused the collapse of a portico upon a large number of workmen, some of whom were killed, though others found refuge in a neighboring church.

Despite this, the project was pursued vigorously. Here we must leave the account to our neutral witness, Ammianus:

> But though Alypius pushed the work forward energetically, and though he was assisted by the governor of the province, frightful balls of flame kept bursting forth near the foundations of the temple, and some were even burned to death. And since the elements persistently drove them back, Julian gave up the attempt.[160]

Profiting from Our Jewish Brothers and Sisters

The events of A.D. 70 and 362 serve as covenant exclamation points that the New Covenant had indeed fulfilled the Old (see CCC 65–66). Yet Catholics should not view these events as reason to celebrate Israel's downfall, lest they endure a much harsher

---

(PG 82); and Gregory Nazianzen, *Orationes IV et V, contra Iulianum* (PG 35).

[160] Ibid., 224–225.

divine judgment themselves.[161] Nor should they invoke events of nearly two thousand years ago to justify virulent prejudices today (see CCC 597–598). Anti-Semitism and anti-Judaism are, in fact, invariably anti-Catholic. As Pope Pius XI noted about Jews and Catholics, "Spiritually, we are all Semites,"[162] the beneficiaries of God's covenant plan to make a universal blessing of the nation of Israel (see Gen. 12:1–2; 22:18)[163] through his Jewish Son (see Matt. 1:1). Jesus himself reminds us that "salvation is from the Jews" (John 4:22), and the biblical story of the Mass incontrovertibly testifies to the privileged role that the Jewish people have played in salvation history (see Rom. 9:3–5).

---

[161] See Vatican II, *Lumen Gentium* ("Dogmatic Constitution on the Church"), no. 14, as cited in Flannery, *Vatican Council II*, 366.

[162] Pope Pius XI, as cited in Pinchas Lapide, *Three Popes and the Jews* (New York: Hawthorn Books, 1967), 114. Pius XI made his remark on September 6, 1938, when he received an ancient and valuable prayer book from Belgian pilgrims. Fittingly, the Pope's words are intimately connected to the biblical story of the Mass, for they were inspired by reading a passage from the Roman Canon, what we today call Eucharistic Prayer I. As Lapide notes, "Opening it on the second prayer after the elevation of the host, the Pope read out to them the passage in which God is besought to accept the altar gifts with the same graciousness in which He once received Abraham's sacrifice. 'Whenever I read the words: The sacrifice of our Father Abraham,' the Pope said, 'I cannot help being deeply moved. Mark well, we call Abraham our Patriarch, our ancestor. Anti-Semitism is irreconcilable with this lofty thought, the noble reality which this prayer expresses.' And, with tears in his eyes, he concluded: 'Anti-Semitism is inadmissible; spiritually, we are all Semites.'"

[163] See Acts 3:25–26.

"Proclaiming the Lord's Death until He Comes"

While the Church speaks of herself as the restored "Israel of God" (see Gal. 6:11–16), God has certainly not abandoned those Jews who continue to adhere to the Old Covenant (see CCC 839–840), even though its sacrifices cannot be offered. He desires them, as he desires all men and women, freely to embrace Christ and his New Covenant as members of his Catholic Church (see CCC 816, 836, 846–856). The Messiah came to save all mankind, particularly those who share his heritage as an Israelite (see Matt. 1:21; 10:6; 15:24; CCC 438, 528).[164] To participate fruitfully in this saving mission to both Jews and the world in general, Catholics en masse must make knowing, living, and sharing their Faith the unambiguous, number-one priority in life that it should be. They must truly seek God's Kingdom first in their lives (see Matt. 6:33), setting aside soul-sapping modern distractions so that they can understand well and passionately convey the biblical story of the Mass.

While Mary, the Pope, and the Eucharist are typically the three major obstacles that prospective converts must overcome, the roles of the Mother of God and the Vicar of Christ are more easily negotiated when seen in light of the foundational, saving work of our Eucharistic Lord. As Pope John Paul II reminds us, the mission of Christ and his Church is primarily conveyed and carried out in the celebration of the Mass:

---

[164] As a Jew who became a Catholic, Fr. Arthur Klyber, C.Ss.R., has written a cogent response for Catholic leaders who discourage evangelization efforts toward Jews: "By what strange Christ-spirit do we suddenly cut off the Lord's own people from the love of their Lord?" (Klyber, *He's a Jew* [New Hope, KY: Remnant of Israel, 1969], 70). Fr. Klyber referred to himself as a "completed Jew."

From the perpetuation of the sacrifice of the Cross and her communion with the body and blood of Christ in the Eucharist, the Church draws the spiritual power needed to carry out her mission. The Eucharist thus appears as both *the source* and *the summit* of all evangelization, since its goal is the communion of mankind with Christ and in him with the Father and the Holy Spirit.[165]

If people come to know and believe in Jesus Christ, and how his saving work is profoundly continued in the Mass, the rest of the doctrinal dominoes will follow. Yet testifying to the Truth in word must be coupled with witnessing to the Word in deed. The example of ancient Israel bears emulating. Ancient Israelites yearned to pierce the veil of the Temple's most holy place, always approaching God with reverential fear. Today, Catholics pierce that veil on a regular basis, yet frequently commune with the Presence of God in the Eucharist in a casual and sometimes irreverent manner. As Pope John Paul II has exhorted, Catholics must become more like the One they worship, reverently offering themselves with Christ's Sacrifice to the Father at Mass; receiving Holy Communion frequently; spending time with their beloved Jesus in Eucharistic adoration; and making regular spiritual communions,[166] so that the world might better know that Jesus is truly Lord. If Catholics begin to see the Mass as the most profound and intimate communion with almighty God that is possible on earth, unworthy reception of the Eucharist will end overnight, liturgical abuses will cease, and the world will be won over to Christ, who will lead us to our ultimate and everlasting

---

[165] Pope John Paul II, *Ecclesia de Eucharistia*, no. 22, emphasis in original, footnote omitted.

[166] Ibid., nos. 10, 13, 25, 34, 42.

communion in the heavenly sanctuary, when the sacramental veil will be removed and we will love our Lord, face-to-face, forever:[167]

Almighty God, help us to live the example of love we celebrate in this eucharist, that we may come to its fulfillment in your presence. We ask this through Christ our Lord. Amen.[168]

Questions for Reflection and Discussion

1. Christian tradition commonly holds that Jesus celebrated his first post-Resurrection Mass at Emmaus. (a) What evidence

---

[167] See 1 Cor. 13:12.

[168] International Commission on English in the Liturgy, *The Roman Missal*, 2nd ed. (New York: Catholic Book Publishing, 1985), "Prayer after Communion," Seventh Sunday in Ordinary Time.

The theologian Fr. François-Xavier Durrwell provides a perceptive insight regarding our appropriation of Christ's Sacrifice in the Mass versus how we will one day appropriate the same sacrificial Lord in heaven. While he comes to us humbly under "the cover" of bread and wine in the Eucharist, he is still fully God in his sacramental coming (*parousia*). It is we, his disciples, Fr. Durrwell notes, who are not fully ready to receive him: "The Eucharist is, for us, an imperfect presence. The imperfection of *parousia* is not the work of the Lord—his Paschal mystery is a total giving of self—it is to be laid at the feet of the Church on earth.... The Church is not able, on this earth, to provide a complete reply to the Christ who comes into it by the giving of himself: the Church is not yet fully matched to the Paschal mystery" (François-Xavier Durrwell, C.Ss.R., "Eucharist and Parousia," *Lumen Vitae* 26 [1971]: 310–311).

from the Bible (see Luke) and other sources, including the *Catechism of the Catholic Church*, supports this position? (b) What two-part, liturgical framework does Jesus apparently illustrate in this sacramental encounter?

2. (a) What do Paul's rhetorical questions in 1 Corinthians 10 suggest about the liturgy that the early Church celebrated? (b) What evidence exists in the passage that the liturgy had a sacrificial nature, despite arguments to the contrary? (c) Why does Paul equate idol worship with devil worship?

3. (a) Why is Paul upset with the Corinthians' immoral conduct at their preliturgical fellowship meal? (b) How does St. Paul's description of the Mass compare with Jesus' at the Last Supper? (c) Paul says that those who unworthily partake of the Communion bread and cup are "guilty of profaning the body and blood of the Lord" (1 Cor. 11:27). In fact, he says that some have gotten sick and even died by doing so (1 Cor. 11:30). How does such biblical evidence support the belief that the Mass is an Offering and partaking of Christ's Body, Blood, Soul, and Divinity?

4. What do the earliest Church writings convey about the primacy of the Lord's Day—and the Mass as its liturgical focus—in the New Covenant?

5. (a) How did Old Covenant worship end in a sorrowful, dramatic fashion, fulfilling the prophecy of Christ? (b) What do the events of A.D. 70 and 362 suggest about the Old and New Covenants? Explain why anti-Semitism and anti-Judaism are incompatible with Catholicism.

6. Why and how must Catholics everywhere make it their mission to learn and live the biblical story of the Mass?

7. In light of what Pope John Paul II has written in his encyclical *Ecclesia de Eucharistia,* how is the Eucharistic Sacrifice crucial to advancing the mission of Christ and his Church?

8. How will heavenly communion be different and superior to Eucharistic Communion?

Appendix

On the Eucharist Offered at the Last Supper as a Completed Sacrifice

In his book *Eucharist and Covenant in John's Last Supper (Jn. 12:44–17:26)*, Msgr. Anthony A. La Femina, S.T.L., J.C.D., argues for the sacramental offering of a completed Sacrifice at the Last Supper. He cites John 13:31, in which Jesus says that he and God the Father have been glorified at the Last Supper:

> One cannot view the eucharistic mystery in a solely human fashion as if it were limited by the categories of time and space.... Before God all the ages of time and space are simultaneously present in their *ontological reality* and not as frames of a motion picture film. The eternity of God indubitably transcends our human understanding because it is part of the mystery that is God himself. However, eternity is not incompatible with time and space any more than God is incompatible with humans or faith is incompatible with created intelligence. . . .
>
> Through its analogous presentation of the Footwashing, the JLSA (Johannine Last Supper Account) indicates both in John 13:1 and John 13:31 that the Eucharist of the Last Supper is a complete sacrifice. It affirms *before*

the Calvary event that Jesus completed his final earthly mission and accomplished the twofold glorification of himself as Messiah and of God as Father. This could only happen because the Eucharist of the Last Supper made ontologically present in a sacramental manner the unique historical reality of Jesus' sacrificial death on Calvary....

John means literally what he wrote in John 13:1 and John 13:31. The sacrifice of Calvary was truly present at the Last Supper in its two component parts: the oblation and the immolation of the victim. In teaching the ontological presence of Calvary at the Last Supper, John affirms the completeness of the sacrificial nature of the Eucharist at that Supper. The Last Supper is precisely where the eucharistic mystery should be contemplated. Calvary "*post-exists*" in the Mass by the identical power by which it "*pre-existed*" at the Last Supper. (57–59, 61, emphasis in original)

While Msgr. La Femina focuses on the death of Christ, as we have learned from our consideration of Christ's fulfillment of the Day of Atonement sacrifices, and as implied in John 13:31, a completed Sacrifice of Calvary made sacramentally present at the Last Supper would necessarily encompass our Lord's glorious Resurrection and Ascension as well. Indeed, it is in the heavenly sanctuary that the Sacrifice of Calvary culminates, and thus the glorification of the Son and the Father as well.

Msgr. La Femina's book has received endorsements from Cardinal Raymond Burke and Father Aidan Nichols, O.P., among other scholars. Said Father Nichols, "The author's thesis is daring and innovative, but eminently compatible with Catholic doctrine. Who would have thought that one could draw from the episode of the Footwashing a view of Eucharistic Sacrifice even bolder than that of the Council of Trent?"

In espousing this "completed Sacrifice" position independent of one another, Msgr. La Femina and I do so in respectful contrast to St. Thomas Aquinas, who argued in the *Summa Theologica* that Jesus' Eucharistic body at the Last Supper was in its pre-Passion/passible form, i.e., capable of suffering: "For it is manifest that the same body of Christ which was then seen by the disciples in its own species, was received by them under the sacramental species. But as seen in its own species it was not impassible; nay more, it was ready for the Passion. Therefore, neither was Christ's body impassible when given under the sacramental species" (*Summa Theologica*, III, Q. 81, art. 3).

Bibliography

Aquinas, St. Thomas. *Summa Theologica*. Vol. 5. Westminster, MD: Christian Classics, 1981.

The Aramaic Bible. Vol. 2 — *Targum Neofiti 1: Exodus*. Translated with introduction and apparatus by Martin McNamara, M.S.C., and notes by Robert Hayward; *Targum Pseudo-Jonathan: Exodus*. Translated with notes by Michael Maher, M.S.C. Collegeville, MN: Liturgical Press, 1994.

Barker, Margaret. "The Temple Roots of the Liturgy," http://www.marquette.edu/maqom/Roots.pdf.

Benin, Stephen D. *The Footprints of God: Divine Accommodation in Jewish and Christian Thought*. Albany, NY: State University of New York Press, 1993.

Boismard, M.-É. *Moses or Jesus: An Essay in Johannine Christology*. Translated by B. T. Viviano. Philadelphia: Fortress Press, 1993.

The Canons and Decrees of the Council of Trent. Translated by Rev. H. J. Schroeder, O.P. Rockford, IL: TAN Books and Publishers, 1978.

Catechism of the Catholic Church, Second Edition. Washington, D.C.: United States Catholic Conference—Libreria Editrice Vaticana, 1994, 1997.

The Catechism of the Council of Trent. Translated by Rev. John A. McHugh, O.P., and Charles J. Callan, O.P. Rockford, IL: TAN Books and Publishers, 1982.

Clark, Stephen B. *Catholics and the Eucharist: A Scriptural Introduction.* Ann Arbor, MI: Servant Publications, 2000.

Daniélou, Jean, S.J. *The Bible and the Liturgy.* Notre Dame, IN: University of Notre Dame Press, 1956.

———. *From Shadows to Reality: Studies in the Biblical Typology of the Fathers.* London: Burns and Oates, 1960.

de Vaux, Roland, O.P. *The Early History of Israel.* Philadelphia: Westminster Press, 1978.

Durrwell, François-Xavier, C.Ss.R. "Eucharist and Parousia." *Lumen Vitae* 26 (1971): 273–315.

Fisher, Eugene, ed. *The Jewish Roots of the Christian Liturgy.* Mahwah, NJ: Paulist Press, 1990.

Flannery, Austin, O.P., ed. *Vatican Council II: The Conciliar and Post Conciliar Documents.* Northport, NY: Costello Publishing, 1975.

Fuller, Rev. Reginald C. et al., eds. *A New Catholic Commentary on Holy Scripture.* Revised and updated edition. Nashville: Thomas Nelson Publishers, 1975.

Gihr, Rev. Dr. Nicholas. *The Holy Sacrifice of the Mass: Dogmatically, Liturgically, and Ascetically Explained.* Translated from the German. St. Louis: B. Herder, 1949.

Bibliography

Gray, Tim. *Mission of the Messiah: On the Gospel of Luke*. Steubenville, OH: Emmaus Road Publishing, 1998.

———. "Where Is the Lamb for the Sacrifice?" *Lay Witness*, March 1977, 4–5.

Hahn, Scott. *A Father Who Keeps His Promises: God's Covenant Love in Scripture*. Ann Arbor, MI: Servant Publications, 1998.

———. *Kinship by Covenant: A Biblical Theological Study of Covenant Types and Texts in the Old and New Testaments*. Ann Arbor, MI: UMI Dissertation Services, 1996.

———. *The Lamb's Supper: The Mass as Heaven on Earth*. New York: Doubleday, 1999.

———. *Understanding Our Father: Biblical Reflections on the Lord's Prayer*. Steubenville, OH: Emmaus Road Publishing, 2002.

Hahn, Scott, and Curtis Mitch. *Ignatius Catholic Study Bible: The Gospel of John*. San Francisco: Ignatius Press, 2003.

———. *Ignatius Catholic Study Bible: The Gospel of Matthew*. San Francisco: Ignatius Press, 2000.

Hamburger, Msgr. Donald C. *The Lamb of God Theme from the Bible*. Columbia, SC: self-published.

Hayward, Robert. "The Present State of Research into the Targumic Account of the Sacrifice of Isaac." *Journal of Jewish Studies* 32 (1981): 127–150.

Jeremias, Joachim. *The Eucharistic Words of Jesus*. Translated by Rev. Arnold Ehrhardt. Oxford, UK: Basil Blackwell, 1955.

John Paul II, Pope. *Ecclesia de Eucharistia*, "On the Eucharist in Its Relationship to the Church." Boston: Pauline Books and Media, 2003.

Jungmann, Rev. Josef A., S.J. *The Mass: An Historical, Theological, and Pastoral Survey.* Translated by Rev. Julian Fernandes, S.J. Edited by Mary Ellen Evans. Collegeville, MN: Liturgical Press, 1976.

————. *The Mass of the Roman Rite: Its Origins and Development.* Replica ed. Allen, TX: Christian Classics, 1986.

Jurgens, William A. *The Faith of the Early Fathers.* Vol. 1. Collegeville, MN: Liturgical Press, 1970.

Keating, Karl. *Catholicism and Fundamentalism: The Attack on "Romanism" by "Bible Christians."* San Francisco: Ignatius Press, 1988.

Kitchen, K. A. On *the Reliability of the Old Testament.* Grand Rapids, MI: Eerdmans, 2003.

Klyber, Rev. Arthur B. C.Ss.R. *He's a Jew.* New Hope, KY: Remnant of Israel, 1969.

————. *Once a Jew . . .* New Hope, KY: Remnant of Israel, 1973.

————. *This Jew: A Book for Christians and Jews about the Crucifixion of Jesus.* New Hope, KY: Remnant of Israel, 1969.

Kurtz, J. H. Martin. *Offerings, Sacrifices and Worship in the Old Testament.* Translated by James Martin. Peabody, MA: Hendrickson Publishers, 1998.

La Femina, Msgr. Anthony A., S.T.L., J.C.D., *Eucharist and Covenant in John's Last Supper (Jn. 12:44–17:26).* New Hope, KY: New Hope Publications, 2000.

Lapide, Pinchas. *Three Popes and the Jews.* New York: Hawthorn Books, 1967.

Bibliography

Lawler, Philip F. "A Principle Rejected." *Catholic World Report*, March 1997.

Léon-Dufour, Fr. Xavier, S.J. *Sharing the Eucharistic Bread: The Witness of the New Testament.* Translated by Matthew J. O'Connell. Mahwah, NJ: Paulist Press, 1987.

Likoudis, James, and Kenneth D. Whitehead. *The Pope, the Council, and the Mass.* West Hanover, MA: Christopher Publishing House, 1981.

Meagher, Father James. *How Christ Said the First Mass.* New York: Christian Press Association Publishing, 1906. Reprinted by TAN Books and Publishers, Rockford, IL.

McCarthy, Dennis J., S.J. *Treaty and Covenant.* Rome: Pontifical Biblical Institute, 1963.

McKenzie, John L., S.J. *Dictionary of the Bible.* New York: Collier Books, MacMillan Publishing, 1965.

McNamara, M., M.S.C., "Melchizedek: Gen 14:17–20 in the Targums, in Rabbinic and Early Christian Literature." *Biblica* 81 (2001): 1–31, as given on http://www.bsw.org/biblica/vol-81-2000/melchizedek-gen-14-17-20-in-the-targums-in-rabbinic-and-early-christian-literature/276/.

McReynolds, Paul R. *Word Study Greek-English New Testament.* Wheaton, IL: Tyndale House, 1998.

Merrill, Eugene H. *Kingdom of Priests: A History of Old Testament Israel.* Grand Rapids, MI: Baker Books, 1997.

O'Connor, Rev. James T. *The Hidden Manna: A Theology of the Eucharist.* San Francisco: Ignatius Press, 1988.

Orchard, Dom Bernard, et al., eds. *A Catholic Commentary on Holy Scripture*. New York: Thomas Nelson and Sons, 1953.

Orlov, Andrei A. "Noah's Younger Brother: The Anti-Noachic Polemics in 2 Enoch." As given at http://www.marquette.edu/maqom/noah.html.

Paul VI, Pope. *Credo of the People of God*. As given in Msgr. Eugene Kevane, ed. *Teaching the Catholic Faith Today: Twentieth Century Catechetical Documents of the Holy See*. Boston: Daughters of St. Paul, 1982.

————. *Mysterium Fidei*, "Encyclical on the Holy Eucharist." September 3, 1965. http://w2.vatican.va/content/paul-vi/en/encyclicals/documents/hf_p-vi_enc_03091965_mysterium.html.

Ratzinger, Joseph Cardinal. *The Spirit of the Liturgy*. Translated by John Saward. San Francisco: Ignatius Press, 2000.

Ray, Stephen K. *Crossing the Tiber: Evangelical Protestants Discover the Historic Church*. San Francisco: Ignatius Press, 1997.

Ricciotti, Giuseppe. *Julian the Apostate*. Translated by M. Joseph Costelloe, S.J. Milwaukee: Bruce Publishing, 1960.

Roberts, Alexander, and James Donaldson. *Ante-Nicene Fathers*. Vol. 1. Peabody, MA: Hendrickson Publishers, 1994.

Roman Missal. 2nd typical ed. New York: Catholic Book Publishing, 1985.

Roman Missal. 3rd typical ed. New York: Catholic Book Publishing, 2010.

Scheeben, Matthias Joseph. *The Mysteries of Christianity*. Translated by Cyril Vollert. St. Louis, MO: B. Herder, 1946.

Bibliography

Shea, Mark. *This Is My Body: An Evangelical Discovers the Real Presence*. Front Royal, VA: Christendom Press, 1993.

Sheed, Frank. *Theology and Sanity*. 2nd ed. San Francisco: Ignatius Press, 1993.

———. *Theology for Beginners*. Ann Arbor, MI: Servant Books, 1982.

———. *What Difference Does Jesus Make?* Huntington, IN: Our Sunday Visitor, 1974.

Sheen, Archbishop Fulton J. *Calvary and the Mass*. New York: P. J. Kenedy and Sons, 1936; retypeset and republished by Coalition in Support of *Ecclesia Dei,* 1996.

Sheler, Jeffery L. "Is the Bible True?: Extraordinary Insights from Archaeology and History." *U.S. News and World Report*, October 25, 1999.

Stravinskas, Peter. *The Catholic Church and the Bible*. 2nd ed. San Francisco: Ignatius Press, 1996.

———. *The Catholic Response*. Huntington, IN: Our Sunday Visitor, 1985.

Stravinskas, Rev. Peter M. J., with Henry Dieterich. *Understanding the Sacraments: A Guide for Prayer and Study*. San Francisco: Ignatius Press, 1997.

The Steubenville Register. "Church Attendance Is Up, but Still Down." January 16, 2004.

Swetnam, Fr. James, S.J. "Christology and the Eucharist in the Epistle to the Hebrews." *Biblica 70* (1989): 74–95.

Vanhoye, Albert, S.J. *Old Testament Priests and the New Priest: According to the New Testament*. Translated by J. Bernard

Orchard, O.S.B. Petersham, MA: St. Bede's Publications, 1986.

Vermes, Geza. "Redemption and Genesis XXII." *Scripture and Tradition in Judaism: Haggadic Studies*. 2nd ed. Leiden, Netherlands: Brill, 1973.

Zodhiates, Spiros, ed. *The Hebrew-Greek Key Study Bible*, New American Standard Bible version. Chattanooga, TN: AMG Publishers, 5990.

Indices

Scripture Index

Scripture Index

Catechism of the Catholic Church Index

General Index

food, multiplied, 132–134,
159–160, 159n100, 196
"forever" meanings
eternity and, 28, 68, 71
everlasting, 149, 221
immortality, 20, 88, 96–97,
138, 145
lifelong, 46
in "ordinance forever," 67–71,
75, 96, 123–124, 163,
180n120, 181
Passover ordinance as, 71,
96, 123, 163, 180n120,
181
salvation as, 7, 29, 47,
156n98, 163, 179–183
until covenant is fulfilled,
67–68, 143, 180n120
until the end of time, 67–68,
180, 180n120
See also "once for all"
forty (number), 79, 133, 145

G

Gabriel, 129, 153
Gallup survey, 4n5
Gemarah, 76n46
Gentiles, 40–41, 114n78, 115,
151–152, 151n95, 155n97,
156n98
Gihr, Rev. Dr. Nicholas, 177,
177n118

glorified body of Christ,
144–145, 162, 173–174,
190–197, 193n136, 204
goats, 28, 34, 77–78, 92,
122–124, 158, 175
See also bulls; lambs
God
Abraham's faith tested by,
53n29, 54–60, 119
acceptance of offerings, 34,
151–152, 176, 183–189,
186n127
as covenantal partner,
52–54, 53n29, 58–59, 68,
107–108
Jesus as, 10n10, 85, 94, 159
obedience to, 17–18, 22,
27–28, 47, 59–60, 75, 98,
178
plan of, 79–80, 175–177
Gray, Tim, 58n32
Greek terms, 95, 114, 137, 159–
160, 159n100, 208, 212–213
Gregory Nazianzen, 216
Gregory the Great, Pope St., 189
Guitmund of Aversa, 198

H

Hagar, 54, 55, 56
Hahn, Scott, 53n29, 109–110
Hallel song, 162
Hayward, Robert, 59nn34–35,
69n38, 70n40, 121n85

General Index

General Index

Temple precursor, 78n49, 106, 155n97

   in the wilderness, 45–46, 77–78, 106, 116–117, 155n97, 213

Tacitus, 66n37, 161

Talmud, 76n46, 93n62

Tamid sacrifices

   Aqedah remembrance of, 119–121

   Eucharist prefigured by, 106, 119–121, 121n87

   ineffectiveness of, 80–88, 113–114, 123–124, 158, 163, 175

Targums, 41n21. 59n34, 68–69, 70n41, 119–121, 120n83, 121n87, 165n105

Temple

   destruction of, 68, 111, 151, 215–217

   Holy of Holies, 78–81, 78n48, 81n51, 117–118, 122, 174–175, 175n113, 220

   service at, 46, 148, 151

   tabernacle and, 78n49, 106, 116, 152, 213

   veil of the, 79, 81n9, 116, 209

Ten Commandments, 66, 106, 122, 134, 210

"tent of meeting." *See* wilderness tabernacle

Tertullian, 161, 161n102

Thomas Aquinas, St., 183n27

   Torah (Pentateuch), 76n46, 172

transubstantiation, 4n5, 6n7, 95, 142–145, 155–162, 193–196, 193n136

   See also Real Presence

Trent, Council of

   on limits of human understanding, 197, 197n141

   on Mass as unbloody offering of Christ's Sacrifice, 87

   on Old Testament offerings fulfilled in Christ, 17n5

   on unworthy priests, 186n127

   whole Christ in each form, 193nn135–136, 195, 198

twelve (number), 57, 107–108, 134, 159, 164n107, 212

U

unity

   Calvary as uniting heaven and earth, 30, 186n127, 189, 207

   Catholic Church and, 30, 186n127, 189, 205–207

   Davidic kingdom restored, 111–113, 142, 148–155, 149n94, 169, 219

   hypostatic union, 191, 195

About the Author

Tom Nash has served the Church for twenty-five years, including as a theology adviser at EWTN and Director of Special Projects at Catholics United for the Faith (CUF). He has been a panelist on *EWTN Theology Roundtable* and co-host of the EWTN series *The Biblical Story of the Mass*. Tom is also a co-author of *Catholic for a Reason III: Scripture and the Mystery of the Mass* (Emmaus Road Publishing).

An Invitation

Reader, the book that you hold in your hands was published by Sophia Institute Press. Sophia Institute seeks to nurture the spiritual, moral, and cultural life of souls and to spread the Gospel of Christ in conformity with the authentic teachings of the Roman Catholic Church.

Our press fulfills this mission by offering translations, reprints, and new publications that afford readers a rich source of the enduring wisdom of mankind.

We also operate two popular online Catholic resources: CrisisMagazine.com and CatholicExchange.com.

Crisis Magazine provides insightful cultural analysis that arms readers with the arguments necessary for navigating the ideological and theological minefields of the day. *Catholic Exchange* provides world news from a Catholic perspective as well as daily devotionals and articles that will help you to grow in holiness and live a life consistent with the teachings of the Church.

In 2013, Sophia Institute launched Sophia Institute for Teachers to renew and rebuild Catholic culture through service to Catholic education. With the goal of nurturing the spiritual, moral, and cultural life of souls, and an abiding respect for the role and work of teachers, we strive to provide materials and programs that are at once enlightening to the mind and ennobling to the heart; faithful and complete, as well as useful and practical.

www.SophiaInstitute.com
www.CatholicExchange.com
www.CrisisMagazine.com
www.SophiaInstituteforTeachers.org